Flower Arranging

FRESH WAYS WITH FLOWERS

Flower Arranging

SUSAN CONDER · SUE PHILLIPS · PAMELA WESTLAND

Longmeadow Press

Acknowledgements

Caroline Arber 37*(BR)*, 89*(T)*; John Bouchier 74;
Camera Press 8*(L,R)*, 10; Chris Crofton 93*(B)*;
E.W.A. 9, 11, 12, 15, 86, 88, 89*(BL)* 90*(BR)*, 91*(BR)*, 92*(BR)*,
94*(BR)*, 95*(TL)*; Fine Art Photographic Library 85*(TL)*;
Will Giles *(Artwork)* 22; Nelson Hargreaves 2, 16, 17, 18, 19, 27,
28, 31, 32, 33*(TL)*, 34, 35, 36, 37*(BL)*, 38, 39, 43, 44, 50,
51, 53, 54, 55, 56, 57, 69, 70, 71, 73, 75*(TL)*, 80, 81, 82, 83*(B)*,
90*(BL)*, 91*(BL)*, 92*(TR)*, 95*(BL)*;
I.G.D.A. 84; Insight 29*(B)* 45*(TL)*; James Jackson 21*(T)*;
Jahres Zeiten Verlag 29*(T)*; Ken Kirkwood 87, 94*(TR)*;
Roy McMahon 20, 33*(BL)*, 33*(BC)*, 52, 72*(L)*, 77, 78, 79, 85*(TR)*;
Mondadori Press 83*(T)*; Jayne Pickering *(Artwork)* 65*(B)*, 76;
Sandra Pond/Will Giles *(Artwork)* 60; Sandra Pond 46;
Smallcombe 3, 21, 23, 24, 25, 40, 41, 47, 48, 49, 59, 61, 62,
63, 65*(TR)*, 66, 67; Syndication International 91*(T)*, 93, 95*(BR)*.

The publishers are grateful for the help of the folowing:
Gail Armitage, Annabel Carter, Laura Lee, John and Bett Wareing.

The material in this book was originally published in 1988 by Orbis Publishing Limited.

This 1991 edition published by Longmeadow Press,
201 High Ridge Road, Stamford, CT 06904

ISBN 0 681 41038 8

Produced by Mandarin Offset
Printed and bound in Hong Kong
0 9 8 7 6 5 4 3 2 1

Contents

Introduction

An arrangement of flowers is always appreciated, bringing fragrance, light and colour into any room in the home. It brings joy to everyone who sees it. If you've never tried arranging flowers because you feel it would be too time consuming and complicated, this book shows just how simple, straightforward and enjoyable the art can be.

Each aspect of flower arranging is clearly explained to give the best possible results. One of the most important points for flower arrangers to remember is that the actual placing of your displays is vital. Do not just put flowers on the nearest available table: in this book you will discover alternative ideas with specific details of how to display flowers – from pedestal arrangements to wall displays. Shape and scale also play an integral role in floral compositions. Many ideas are featured here, such as shaping arrangements to fit awkward spaces and exploring proportion from the minute to the expansive.

The container in which flowers are placed can bring an extra dimension and appeal to a display. Ordinary glass or china vases have their place, but more unusual vessels, such as a hollowed-out fruit or vegetable, can give an arrangement added impact.

Colour in arrangements can be subtle or strident. It can calm or excite, lift the spirits or induce tranquillity. This book shows how to use colour creatively to evoke specific moods.

The book also gives useful information showing how flowers can enhance each and every room of your home, from kitchens to bathrooms, stairways to bedrooms.

Once you have grasped the few basic guidelines, you can use the ideas here as a stepping-stone to fulfil your own floral fantasies. The innovations explored in the section on advanced ideas will encourage you to be more adventurous in your approach and help you tap your own ingenuity.

To make it easier to create stunning arrangements such as those illustrated in the book, many displays have step by step photographs that demonstrate clearly how to make them.

All flowers are beautiful, but fresh flowers have a particular vibrance and style. Every arrangement in this book will show you the way to maximize their exquisite potential.

Enjoying Fresh Flowers

THE RIGHT FLOWERS IN THE RIGHT SETTING: THAT'S THE ART OF SUCCESSFUL FLOWER ARRANGING.

The strong sunshine golds and yellows of decorative grasses, chrysanthemums, gaillardia and lilies show how flowers can give a 'lift' to a dark room corner. (BELOW LEFT)

As a complete contrast, blue flowers combined with lush green foliage create a cool and restful effect, suitable for a sitting room or bedroom. This arrangement features cornflowers, deep blue freesias and different textured leaves. (BELOW RIGHT)

A floral arrangement can enhance your home. Flowers also say something about you, and each time they are admired, so too is your handiwork, artistry and skill. The advantage of flower arrangements is that they are versatile and infinitely changeable. New designs can be created every few days, or long-lasting displays re-arranged to look fresh and original. Flowers can be chosen and styled to suit specific rooms or areas, to evoke a 'mood', or to complement a special occasion.

THE IMPORTANCE OF PLANNING

Planning a display does not mean sticking rigidly to a formal design. In today's busy households 'over-arranged' flowers look out of place. Wise planning is working out the right size and shape for a display; knowing which colours and flowers go well together, and choosing appropriate containers.

Keep in mind, too, the size and shape of an arrangement. It should fit in with the proportions of the room. For example, tall bunches of lilies suit big, wide rooms, while in small rooms dainty arrangements are most effective. Plan your displays to suit the time you can devote to them – and the time you need them to last. Long-lasting flowers such as carnations, chrys-

anthemums and orchids are ideal if you only find time to create a hallway or dining room arrangement once a week.

PRACTICAL AND PRETTY
While showing off flowers to their best advantage, make sure that they will not be 'in the way'. Shallow, water-filled bowls brimming with bobbing blossoms, for example, are the least appropriate arrangement for a children's party, but make perfect table decorations for a celebratory dinner. And tumbling, trailing flowers would be unwise on a narrow mantelpiece but just right on a wide sideboard.

SIZING AND STYLING
Before buying or cutting flowers, roughly work out the size and shape of your display. If you are planning to put a tall arrangement in a narrow alcove, for example, you might decide that the flowers you intend to use would look cramped or out of proportion in the available space. A

successful arrangement harmonizes with its surroundings. To achieve harmony, study the room where the arrangement is to go, taking into account the colours and atmosphere. A look that works well in one situation will not necessarily succeed in another. For example, a stark 'minimalist' Japanese-style arrangement won't suit a traditional sitting room at all, but would look right in a deliberately barely-furnished, modern room-setting. Similarly, a large, colourful display would look out of place in the modern room, but would 'belong' in a more traditional one. However magnificent an arrangement, it won't look good unless it suits its surroundings.

CHOOSING THE RIGHT CONTAINERS
The right vase or container can bring an arrangement to life. Many types of varying containers can be used: china jugs, antique chamber pots, teapots, pretty mugs, shells, bottles — the list is endless.

Soft sunlight filters through a group of apricot, lemon and white lilies and chrysanthemums. Small arrangements of similar flowers are placed on occasional tables placed on occasional tables beside the sofa and chairs - a pretty personal touch emphasizing how flowers enhance your home. (ABOVE)

PLACING FLOWERS IN YOUR HOME

Always take time when deciding where to place an arrangement for maximum effect.

The cool elements of this marble and glass table are accentuated by an arrangement of white flowers and green foliage which maximizes the beauty of this dining room. (BELOW)

Flowers can be as much part of your room design as your furniture – they can offer as much pleasure and comfort to the eye and mind as can a deep-seated sofa to the body. A room without flowers and plants can seem sterile, even hostile – fresh flowers add colour and beauty and make a room feel lived in. A few simple vases can complement existing decor or transform dull surroundings by emphasising attractive features.

To make flowers part of your home, you need to consider them in relation to the furniture and ornaments and how they tone or contrast with fabrics, wall coverings and carpets. Form, line and scent as well as choice of containers also have to be taken into account.

Thinking about these factors before you visit the florist is part of the pleasure of flower arranging.

CHANGING THE MOOD

If you have a very formal room with long Georgian windows, elegant furniture and accessories, soften the formality and introduce a more light-hearted atmosphere into the room by adding flowers. Alleviate muted tones with creamy yellow flowers – delicate spiky varieties that give height, such as fennel.

By simply adding flowers, the mood of the room will have been transformed from austerity into abundance. Flowers will make it a room that invites its inhabitants to be happy. Your choice of furniture will have to last for several years and even changing your colour scheme is expensive and time-consuming. By moving your furniture about periodically and adding fresh flowers, you can transform your room.

Look at your room carefully. Make a group of your favourite vases on the floor and consider where you might put them if you altered the position of your furniture. Be flexible in your approach and try to see objects and colours in a fresh light. Do this literally by moving an occasional table under a hanging lamp and putting a bowl of roses in the pool of light, or by changing the position of standard lamps or the angles of spotlights to draw attention to your flowers.

One of the most popular rooms for

flowers is the dining room and the focus of any dining room is its table. A large polished expanse of wood with nothing on it has a clinical appearance. Your unused table can be used for a spectacular display which can be enjoyed from whichever side it is viewed.

Choose your containers first and take your cue from the furnishings. Glass containers might best suit a reflective table top. If there is a window nearby, make the most of the sunlight, glass, water and reflected light. Avoid heavy blooms that block the light and choose fluffy or spiky flowers, variegated grasses and fern fronds. You will need only a few in each container. A few delicate blooms will look more relaxed and, placed together in several arrangements, will create a haze of light and colour.

A GLORIOUS CONTRAST
Many interiors decorated in the styles of the last 15 years are in neutral colours which are restful and never date. However, sometimes these neutral surroundings need pepping up.

If your furnishings are mainly stone, grey, oatmeal and cream, with a hint of pink, draw out the pink tones. Add some palms in terracotta pots and scatter terracotta-coloured chintz cushions to warm up the natural background. Small jars and earthenware dishes on coffee tables and side tables can brim with bunches of nasturtiums and marigolds.

ARCHITECTURAL SIMPLICITY
In a traditional-style room with a wealth of detail – floral furnishings, heavy curtains,

The careful arrangement of the furniture in this living room means that the bold tones of the spectacular Japanese screen are thrown into dramatic relief by the mass of bird of paradise flowers set in a simple goldfish bowl. (ABOVE)

11

A traditional room furnished with a period chest of drawers and old master painting receives a splash of vibrancy from this display featuring full-blown red roses. (RIGHT)

pictures, mirrors and architectural features – an abundance of flowers fits in easily. Modern rooms can be more difficult to cater for, with their accent on space instead of clutter, sparse furnishing without frills and plain blinds in place of curtains.

The furnishings are usually chunky, with definite edges and angles. They call for vases with emphatic proportions and classic shapes: cylinders, tubes, bowls and boxes. Opt for austere, architecturally simple flowers such as arum lilies or anthuriums.

Many modern furnishing fabrics feature irregular stripes, either herringbone or bold straight lines or free-form lines. These are all ideas taken from nature – variegated leaves, striped flowers and dappled sunlight. It is simple to re-introduce these ideas into your flower arrangements and the combinations that you create will look stunning.

You could introduce variegated leaves and grasses into your vases and keep the colours muted. Try an all-green arrangement for a strikingly modern display. Green bells of Ireland, hops, eucalyptus, variegated ivy, hypericum and green hydrangea can team dramatically with feathery grasses and leafy branches.

MIX AND MERGE

Bedrooms are for relaxation. Flowers in the bedroom should be soothing and restful. Take your cue from your furnishings and let them dictate the colours of your flowers. If you have a luxurious bedroom, highlight the opulence by placing your main flower arrangement in a tall cut-glass vase in front of the mirror and complement it with candles or intimate lamplight. For the bedside tables choose the same flowers, but cut the stems very short and float them in low, shallow bowls. This guards against them being knocked over in the night. When possible, choose flowers that have a wonderful perfume, but make sure that the fragrance is subtle or the effect will be too overpowering. Freesias, for instance, are perfect flowers in bedrooms.

The pretty peach bedroom walls are complemented by a low arrangement of orange lilies on the bedside table, producing a warm, intimate glow. (LEFT)

The dramatic blooms of glossy red anthuriums and the tall, rigid bulrushes arranged in a bold black vase make a startling impact among the strong hues of this masculine modern-style bedroom. (LEFT)

PEDESTAL ARRANGEMENTS

Give your flowers a lift by creating simple pedestal displays along traditional or informal lines.

The pedestal arrangement is a traditional English flower design and is most frequently seen on formal occasions. This should not put off the inexperienced floral arranger; pedestal designs are not difficult to construct and, if you do not own a pedestal container, they can be easily improvised from household objects.

Using a pedestal does have considerable advantages over placing stems in a vase. When the plant material is raised above a surface and the stems are anchored in foam as they are in a pedestal design, you can create a variety of design shapes with flowing, downward-sweeping lines, and what is known as 'movement'. By so doing, you produce space around the container and beneath the flowers, which adds lightness to the design and creates an imposing overall effect.

Once you understand and master the technique of elevating flowers, you will discover that there are many creative ways to display them. You could create a triangular design of glowing daffodils and spring flowers which appears to hover just above a reflective polished wooden table, or a cascade of foliage and freesias spilling over the sides of a tall, shiny candlestick.

Pedestals come in all shapes and sizes and, for practical purposes, the term can be applied to any container which raises arrangements even a little above a table top or any other surface.

CREATING PEDESTAL CONTAINERS

The most important requirement of a pedestal container is that you can fix to its top a holder containing wet florist's foam.

The obvious choice for an improvised pedestal is any item with a small raised stem, for example, a cake stand, an old-fashioned ham plate, a fruit bowl, a stemmed wine glass or a grapefruit glass. Alternatively, you can create stands on which to place a holder filled with flowers. Such objects include tall, slender vases, wine carafes and straight-sided tumblers.

Candlesticks make perfect pedestals. They allow you to create lovely, cascading designs and take up a minimum table space.

Although much larger, the base of a standard lamp can also be used as a pedestal for flower arrangements. This is especially useful to enhance rooms that have cluttered surfaces, but lack a raised decorative focus.

A FIRM FOUNDATION

The most important factor in creating a pedestal design is balancing the arrangement. This involves a meticulous approach to all stages of construction, from securing the foam or water-holding container to using more or less equal weight of material at the front and back of the design.

The size and type of your pedestal will determine the most suitable type of foam holder to use. When using fresh flowers, the holder needs to be large and deep enough to hold a cylinder or block of foam, with space to spare for topping up with water daily. Such a holder can be anything from an upturned jar lid fitted on to the top of a small candlestick to a baking dish on a floor-standing pedestal or tall stool.

CONCEALING THE MECHANICS

In general, foam-holders are purely functional and can be completely concealed by large leaves, sprays and short-stemmed flowers placed close against the foam.

If you wish to use a tall, slender vase with a neck about 7.5-10cm (3-4in) in diameter as a pedestal, it is best to fit it with a shallow, plastic 'candlecup' holder,

The base of an old floor lamp is here cleverly used as a pedestal device which lifts a beautiful basket of flowers in a living room where there is little table space available. (LEFT)

A bright pedestal-style arrangement of orange lilies and carnations, irises and gnarled twigs proves that not all pedestal designs need be formal, and gives inspiration to experiment with different styles of arranging. (RIGHT)

available from florists. Press about three small pieces of extra-tacky florist's adhesive clay on to the container's rim, then press the plastic holder firmly in place. Position a piece of soaked foam in the holder and tape it in place with a criss-cross of florist's adhesive tape, taking the tape over the foam, down both sides, on to and under the candlecup, and finally fixing it to the sides of the vase.

The larger the container, the heavier the burden of plant materials it can bear. Allow for this when securing the foam. Fix a large, dry container or shallow tray to the top of a pedestal with several substantial dabs of clay and attach two or three prongs to the base with more clay. Press the soaked foam on to these spikes – and then tape them in place. For extra

security, cover it with a piece of lightly-crushed chicken wire, and secure this with wire taken over and around the foam, under the container, and on to the pedestal.

A triangular floral design is well suited to a raised position and is by far the most simple flower arrangement to create on a pedestal.

JUDGING PROPORTIONS

For the shape and the container to look in proportion, it is important to judge correctly, and to establish first, the length of the central stem that determines the vertical height or, in a predominantly horizontal design, the length of the side stems. In both cases, these leading stems should be at least one-and-a-half times the height (or width) of the pedestal. If you are using a long, lean coffee pot, it is the height you measure. If you use a cake plate on a shallow stand, it is the width that is the crucial measurement. For the extreme points of a triangle design use foliage.

For the most natural look, aim to make it look as if all the stems 'grow' from one central position, the vertical ones rising up and the lower side ones slanting down from that point.

Having composed the triangular outline with foliage, conceal the container and foam with a few large leaves. Lastly, position the flowers. As a rule of thumb, try to get the largest flowers at the centre of the arrangement and the slimmest at the edges. Be sure to have some long-stemmed flowers coming well forward

from the centre. This adds light and air to the design and creates the most natural and pleasing look.

As you work on your arrangement, check it from all the angles from which it will be viewed. Don't forget that flower arrangements have three dimensions, not one, so you should aim to create a good balance and depth. The process of achieving this starts when you place the first flowers, outlining the shape of the arrangement and establishing the general proportion. And it continues right through to when you position the less important flowers and foliage that you are using to fill out the arrangement. Remember to vary the angle at which you place each flower it will create an arrangement with more interesting texture and make all the difference to the final effect.

A free-standing pedestal cascading with trails of spring-flowering broom is placed by a lattice window where it will create maximum impact. The pink and yellow are echoed in the ranunculus and sprays of alstroemeria. (LEFT)

17

WALL DISPLAYS

When the table's in use and all the shelves are full to overflowing, there's one place left that has endless potential, the walls of every room.

Think of the walls in your home as a background for your flowers; a huge blank canvas which you can 'paint' with flower compositions designed either to hang on the walls or to be viewed against them.

Few walls are completely blank so take into account the wallpaper, colour, texture, pattern and style when planning arrangements. Imagine a delicate, small bunch of flowers, for instance, against a rough brick wall; the flowers would be completely over-shadowed by the wall's craggy texture and geometric form. But set the flowers against a flower-speckled wallpaper in the bedroom and it would look just right. Picture, too, a 1930s pottery wall vase. Its swirling design would harmonize perfectly with a pastel-coloured bedroom wall, but be quite out of place against a modern wallpaper.

WALL VASES

Decorative wall vases, which were enormously popular in the early part of this century, have come right back into fashion and now modern versions are quite cheaply available in many shops. You can even find the real thing if you hunt around; try junk shops, charity shops and car boot sales. The original vases are usually cone, horn or shell-shaped, flat on one side, with generously flowing, sculptured lines on the other, and come in delicate pastel shades – often pearl or white but occasionally in wonderful greens, blues and yellows.

Aim to complement the fluid lines of such vases with a flowing, cascading outline etched with foliage and flower stems. Trails of small variegated ivy, of clematis, honeysuckle, periwinkle and lamium will create natural, gentle lines which will act as a guide when you are arranging the flowers. Alstroemeria, Doris pinks, spray pinks, ranunculus, roses, Shirley poppies – these are all in the spirit of the style.

THE RUSTIC LOOK

Florist shops, department stores, basket shops and charity shops all offer a wide selection of country-style flower containers to hang on the walls. Some are like open satchels woven in cane; some are made of plaited reeds and rushes, others are woven with dried fern leaves or moss – and all are beautifully decorative, even without flowers.

Pottery and china wall vases can be treated like any other flower containers, a piece of foam pressed into the aperture to hold the stems. However, these country-look containers are not water-tight and, when they are used for fresh flowers, need a different treatment. Wrap a piece of soaked florist's foam in foil, and push a stub wire through it from side to side. Place the foil parcel in the basket container and push the wire ends through the back of the basket weave, twisting them over to hold the foam in place. Then press

As pretty as a picture over a small dressing table, a white wall vase spills over with trailing eucalyptus leaves, spray pinks and pink alstroemeria. (RIGHT)

woody stems – of evergreen oak leaves, preserved leaves, roses or chrysanthemums, for example – through the foil covering and into the foam. To ease the way for less rigid stems, first push a hole in the foam with a fine metal or wooden skewer.

A word of caution. If your rustic container is made of a thin substance, and if it is to be hung on anything other than a waterproof wall surface, it is best to line the container first with a piece of polythene. Moisture may seep out through the holes made in the foil, and damage the paintwork or wallpaper.

CREATING WALL DESIGNS

Give your creative flair full rein, and design wall decorations based on equally rustic items. You can use rafffia or cane place mats, straw fans, shallow wooden boxes as a background for flower compositions. To make freestyle designs within such a 'frame', wire or tape a thin block of foam to the centre or to one side of your chosen hanging base. Plan the size and scale of the design – it might be a nosegay of colourful statice, poppy seedheads and tiny teasels – before cutting the stems. It could be helpful to sketch out the design on paper first.

To create a more formal design of closely-packed flowerheads – such as strawflowers and love-in-a-mist seedheads in concentric rings – cut out a thin piece of foam to fit neatly into the frame, cut the stems to a short, uniform length and press them into the foam. Wooden cheese boxes from a delicatessen are ideal containers for designs of this kind but when using them for fresh flower arrangements, you must of course thoroughly

A long stretch of wall in a passage or garden room becomes a gallery for a fresh flower creation. The Filippino wall container, made of woven fern leaves, brims over with evergreen oak leaves and spray chrysanthemums, their stems held in a piece of soaked (and foil-covered) foam. (ABOVE)

19

A wall-hung basket of vibrant flowers provides a bright display in a room where surface space is limited. (RIGHT)

waterproof them first using a piece of polythene sheeting.

HOOPS, SWAGS AND RIBBONS

There is a long tradition of decorating our homes on festive occasions (and not only at Christmas) with flower garlands of all kinds. Hoops, swags and ribbons of flowers and foliage are beautiful wall decorations, making the time and effort that goes with their creation worthwhile.

Making flower rings is straightforward. You can buy polystyrene rings filled with standard stem-holding foam and once the foam is wet press stems randomly into the foam, taking care to cover the (often bright green) outer ring.

Ribbons of pale pink and blue flowers and creamy-gold seedheads flanking a mirror frame, a garland of fresh flowers

looped over an arch, a hoop of dainty pink rose-buds and cornflowers hanging over a bedhead or fireplace – these are all wonderful ideas when you have a special occasion and want to decorate your walls.

Hanging garlands on a wall can also be a great way of filling an empty gap, if you haven't any pictures for that particular room. If you are using dried flowers for such a garland, you could also make a simple arrangement from a selection of them, and place it somewhere in the room to compliment the garland.

It's fun to explore all the different ways in which flowers can be displayed on the walls, and whether your choice is elaborate be-ribboned fresh flower garlands or simple, no-fuss dried-flower posies, your unique floral decorations are guaranteed to make the plainest room look that bit more special.

S *unflowers and foliage combine here to make a vivid and eye-catching display in an elegant wrought-iron lantern vase. (LEFT)*

A *wall display in miniature; this compact collection of hyacinths, grape hyacinths and statice in blue would suit a country-style kitchen. (LEFT)*

21

STEP *by* STEP

Wall Display

Most large flower arrangements are placed on a table, shelf or pedestal or even on the floor. Here's a wall-hanging flower display, with easy-to-follow step-by-step instructions, large enough to be the main decorative feature of a room. It is ideal if horizontal space is in short supply.

The oval-shaped, formal arrangement is front facing with densely packed flowers and foliage filling a flat-backed, wicker wall basket. The stems are inserted into a saturated florist's foam block which is concealed within the plastic-lined pouch.

FLOWERS AND FOLIAGE

The colour scheme, based on yellow, green and white, is bright and cheerful. The design calls for strong-shaped flowers which can be seen from across the room; the same varieties of flowers are used in pedestal displays to make an impact from a distance. All the flowers are available commercially. White is the florist's staple colour and you could easily substitute peach or pink for the yellow flowers or deepen the whole scheme with richer yellows, oranges and russets if this suits your room decor better – or if yellow isn't your favourite colour.

Foliage plays a subsidiary, but still important, role in the arrangement, adding height and contrasting form, and serving as a flat backdrop against which the flowers are displayed. Not surprisingly, evergreen foliage is longer lasting than deciduous foliage when cut, and so is ideal. This is not a cheap display, but all the flowers shown are long-lasting, so the composition is good value for money and an ideal arrangement to make if you are having guests. For an even more splendid effect, make a pair of wall-hanging arrangements to put either side of a large mirror, dining-room cabinet, buffet table or sofa.

PREPARING DECORATIVE CONES

You can give the basket extra appeal by decorating it with fir, pine or larch cones. Spray them with leaf shine or anti-static spray to give them a shiny appearance and help stop them accumulating dust. This is important, as you are unlikely to be able to dust them to any great effect when the basket is on the wall. Protect your work surface first.

Wrap medium gauge stub wire around the base of a cone, bending the wire back upon itself to form an artificial stem. Thread the wire through the basket weave to secure it. Tuck in the sharp ends. Repeat for the other cones. Alternatively, attach the cones to the basket with strong, clear adhesive.

Transform an empty stretch of wall into an impressive focal point by filling a flat-backed wicker basket with a magnificent mass of fresh flowers and foliage. (FAR RIGHT)

THE CONTAINER

The unusual wall basket consists of a mat-like circle of woven wicker, 37cm (15in) in diameter, with a rounded, half-circle front pouch and a handle. The basketware sections of department stores and many larger garden centres sell woven wall baskets. If you are planning a special occasion display, it is worth buying two to make a matching pair.

KEEPING FLOWERS FRESH

Do not position the display above a radiator or the flowers will wilt quickly. Incandescent light bulbs also give off heat so keep the arrangement well away from wall lights.

The weight of the saturated florist's foam and flowers is considerable so make sure the support is solid and test it first before putting the whole weight of the display on it. Attach to the wall using rawl plugs or brackets.

Water the florist's foam regularly by standing on a chair and using a long-spouted watering can, if necessary. Also, spray the flowers with a fine mist of fresh water from time to time.

MAKING A BRIGHT WALL DISPLAY

YOU WILL NEED

 1 *2 bunches of chincherinchee*
 2 *6 stems of white gerbera*
 3 *6 stems of white longiflorum lily*
 4 *4 stems of variegated elaeagnus*
 5 *4 stems of yellow spider chrysanthemum*
 6 *4 stems of white daisy chrysanthemum*
 7 *3 stems of yellow gladiolus*
 8 *wall-hanging basket, decorated with cones*
 9 *clear plastic sheeting*
 10 *block of florist's foam*
 11 *knife*

1

2

3

4

5

6

1 Line a wall-hanging basket with a sheet of clear plastic. Fill the basket with a block of pre-soaked florist's foam. Strip the lower leaves from three gladiolus stems then place them vertically side by side at the back of the basket. Fill out the sides with leaves, cut at a slant.

2 Condition the elaeagnus thoroughly before arranging by giving it a long drink of water. Cut the stems so that the tallest stands as high as the gladioli. Insert the taller stems at the back. Position the shorter stems at the front and sides so that some trail over the rim.

3 Cut four stems of yellow spider chrysanthemum into short sprigs and place them at the front of the display. Place two stems of white chrysanthemum in the middle at the front. Leave the other stems longer and insert them on either side of the central gladioli.

4 Strip the lower leaves from six longiflorum lilies and cut the ends at a slant and so that they are at graduated heights; the tallest should be about 7.5cm (3in) shorter than the gladioli. Place in the centre of the arrangement, the flowerheads facing outwards.

5 Introduce six white gerbera stems to the display. Cut all the stems to different lengths. Place four gerbera stems centrally in the arrangement. Position each of the two remaining stems either side of the arrangement.

6 Insert the chincherinchee flowers into the foam, angled so they protrude beyond the other flowers to give a slightly spiky silhouette. Position the flowers so the green tips hang downwards. Check the display from the front, making sure none of the foam is visible.

Floral Shapes and Sizes

WHEN ARRANGING FLOWERS, TAKE NOTE OF THEIR VARIOUS SHAPES AND SIZES AND USE THEM TO BEST EFFECT IN YOUR DISPLAY.

Floral ingredients can be used in various ways to create unusual and striking displays. Change one ingredient for one of another shape and the design appears quite different.

Flowers grow in all shapes and sizes from domes, bell-shaped and trumpet-shaped blooms to umbrella-like domes and soft, fluffy spires. A few are huge and mop-headed and others so tiny that they have a speckly and almost spotty appearance.

Particularly impressive are feature flowers which grow singly, each flower-head balancing perfectly on top of a supporting stem and commanding individual attention. Others, such as sweet peas, grow in a family of six or eight to a stem and form a soft, twirling shape. Many flowering plants, such as golden rod, comprise a multitude of florets which create a magnificent massed effect. Foliage also comes in an assortment of shapes and sizes. There are sharp little needles along a poker-straight stem, round, flat and fleshy leaves, and those that form a dense, almost furry mass.

Even stems contribute their own texture and form. Some are completely straight, others have a gently arching curve. Note their contours carefully when selecting them for more formal crescent and 'S' shaped designs. Certain stems, such as cow parsley, create intricate geometric patterns.

Many stems, such as clematis, twist and twirl in every direction. Use them to create unusual and interesting outlines and trails in flower designs.

BASIC SHAPES

Often the design potential of an unusual-shaped flower, leaf or stem is overlooked. Before arranging, consider how it can compliment the other materials used in the same display. You will create more versatile designs, if you combine plant shapes in your arrangements.

Four basic flower shapes are needed to fulfil most arranging requirements: tall spires of plant material to determine the height and possibly the width of a design; small round flowers to act as fillers; larger trumpet-shaped flowers to provide focal points and give visual weight at the base; and a 'softening' material, such as lady's mantle, to give a slightly blurred look and bridge the changes in flower shapes in the design for a more pleasing effect.

INFORMAL DESIGNS

Choosing plant material with a classic selection of shapes does not restrict you to composing only traditional or formal designs – natural, informal displays are also possible. The exciting aspect of using shapes in arrangements is exploiting the full design potential that exists in every kind of plant material. Each type of leaf and flower can be adapted to suit specific design requirements. You may find that it helps you to rough out the design you have in mind on paper before you start – then you can plan what flowers and foliage you most want to use.

If tall stems are needed to reach from the top to the bottom of a display, choose the material according to the scale of the

The shapes of flowers are as diverse as they are numerous; different combinations can alter radically the shape, scale and, ultimately, the impact of any flower arrangement as shown in this multi-textured arrangement. (FAR RIGHT)

arrangement. For example, use the long, pointed stems of veronica to provide medium height with minimal width.

An effective way of drawing attention to favourite feature flowers, such as soft and pretty old-fashioned roses or multi-petalled poppies, is to surround them with less eye-catching plant material. The nosegay in the opening picture, arranged in a rustic grey-green, rough-textured stone pot, features two roses nestling close against the rim as principal flowers. Their prominence is accentuated through being surrounded by smaller blooms – spray carnations, Doris pinks, corn-flowers and bright little feverfew daisies. The secondary flowers in the group are mallow – deep trumpet-shaped blooms in a colour exactly matching the darker rose. The contrast between slender, curving flowering stems and full-petalled flowers is one which is both interesting to com-pose and attractive to look at. The naturally curving stems of broom – in or out of flower – seem tailor-made to form into a crescent, an arc or an 'S' shape. Position two arched stems curving in different directions on opposite sides of a piece of foam and place in a small, flat rectangular dish. This basic outline forms a classic crescent shape, the tips tapering up elegantly on each side. Position two broom, clematis, ivy or other stems that already have a double curve, one reaching up and one curving down from the top of a tall container to form a lazy 'S' shape. In flower arranging terms, and if the ultimate shape were regular and recognizable, such a display would be known as a 'Hogarth curve'. All that is needed to complete such a design is a few stems to follow and emphasize the outline curves and a cluster of solid flowers to provide visual weight at the base.

*R*oses form a central cluster while spray carnations and sweet peas taper off at the tips of this hat-band decoration. Tiny gypsophila flowers add contrast. (RIGHT)

*T*he slender, deep-green
stems of bear grass
cascade from the glass vase like
a fountain around a collection of
mallow, godetia and other
garden flowers. The overall
effect is thus informal. (ABOVE)

A huge, pale-pink,
papery-petalled poppy
takes visual precedence over
smaller, brighter flowers. These
are arranged in the background
to form a continuous framing
band. (LEFT)

USING SHAPE CREATIVELY

Experiment with patterns and shapes, rather than simply placing fresh flowers in an ordinary vase.

Move away from the well-known, conventional forms of flower arrangements and experiment with exciting patterns and shapes. Take a round, square or rectangular shallow container and arrange flowers in a geometric, patchwork style; use any of the available foam shapes to make cones, rings and spheres of flowers or create your own fantasy shapes to make original and exotic floral decorations.

RINGS AND HOOPS

Rings and hoops are traditional shapes for flower and foliage designs. Among the prettiest are those with a pastoral feel to them, made from a bunch of meadow grasses twisted casually into a hoop of stems and ears that is slightly asymmetrical. You can choose a more formal style by using foam rings or craggy hoops of twisted branches and then decorating them afterwards.

There are two types of foam ring commercially available for use with fresh materials. One of the fresh-flower types consists of a rigid plastic ring filled with florist's foam. The other absorbent type of ring is made of soft polystyrene, fused to the foam to make a complete – and non-re-usable – unit. Both of these types can be soaked with water and used with short stems of exotic or country flowers to make lovely wall and table decorations.

SPECIAL OCCASION RINGS

With an absorbent foam ring, which will keep flowers and leaves fresh for several days, you can create floral circlets to suit every kind of occasion. You can go for a romantic look with tiny roses, tendrils of sweet peas and snippings of lady's mantle, or choose a more natural style and fill the ring with pink and white campion, wild cow parsley flowers and bright green shoots of dead-nettle. Or, for a cool-looking display, you could cover the ring with a selection of pale-coloured and variegated foliage, green nicotiana and euphorbia, and add a few white flowers to highlight the other colours.

CHANGING THE SHAPE

A basic ring shape can be transformed into a horseshoe or a crescent simply by cutting out a segment. This is easy to do with a polystyrene and absorbent foam ring. The type that's enclosed in a brittle plastic casing will probably need to be cut with a small hand saw.

If you prefer not to use any of the ready-made shapes, you can make your own ring base from thickly plaited raffia, dried plant stems or from a bent wire coathanger. If using the latter, bind handfuls of sphagnum moss on to the wire structure to thicken it out and soften the appearance. If the flowers and leaves don't cover the ring completely, it won't matter as it will be covered with natural-looking moss.

FLOWER CIRCLETS

This type of design, a grass ring speckled with brilliant flowers, comes from France. Young girls wear circlets like this on the backs of their heads or around a straw hat when they take part in village festivals.

This way of decorating a summer hat is not suitable for every occasion, however. For a glamorous event, such as a wedding, a straw hat decorated with a cluster of pretty, open flowers is more appropriate. Partly opened roses, carnations, pinks, feverfew and sweet peas with gypsophila would make a lovely mixture of shapes and textures.

Measure a piece of ribbon long enough to go round the hat brim, with enough left over to tie in a knot and leave trailing ends. Cut the flowers and keep them in water until the last minute. Just before the event, wire, staple, pin or sew them to the band and spray the flowers lightly with water to keep them fresh.

A ring of wheat makes a pretty, contrasting frame for a selection of bright fresh flowers. (FAR RIGHT)

Everyday containers such as a shoe box and a plastic tub get a facelift with a moss covering. Make different shapes with rings or rows of flowers. (RIGHT)

FLORAL CONES

Floral rings may be the most adaptable and versatile of shapes, but they aren't the only ready-made ones you can buy. Florists sell cone shapes of both absorbent and dry foam, which you can use as a base for tight, spiral designs of small flowerheads, nuts, cones and seedheads, or as the 'trunk' for an imaginative evergreen tree decoration.

To make a tight design that follows the outline of the cone closely, choose fresh flowers with compact flowerheads. You can enjoy creating the pattern, arranging the flowers in rings, starting from the top with the smallest, neatest materials.

A more ambitious way to cover a cone is with a spiral pattern, the flowers and seedheads twisting around the shape from top to bottom. To achieve an even spiral, pin a piece of string to the top, wind it around the cone and pin it at the base. You can then use this 'plumb-line' guide when you are arranging the first row of materials.

The colourful design (bottom right) resting on a wire cooling rack is one of the easiest ways of arranging flowers into a decorative shape. The featured display uses concentric circles of floral colour, and was created around a quiche dish as well as the wire rack.

FLOWER SPHERES

Spherical shapes can be used to create beautiful indoor 'designer' trees. They can also be used to make floral mobiles — hanging decorations to highlight an alcove or arch. Fresh-flower balls are lovely decorations for a party; dried-flower ones make a more lasting feature. You can enjoy both by arranging fresh grasses and certain flowers in a soaked foam sphere, leaving them to dry out naturally where they hang.

FLOWER SCULPTURE

It can be even more rewarding to devise and cut out your own foam shapes and cover them with flowers. The principle is easy. Take a large block of dry foam and cut it in half lengthways to make a narrow slice. Draw the pattern of your chosen shape on paper, then trace over it on to the foam. The pressure of a pencil or ballpoint pen will leave an imprint. Cut out the shape around the imprint, using a sharp knife. For a large-scale display, stick the foam halves together, widthways or lengthways.

You can cover your foam shape with flowers of a single flower type in a variety of colours to define different parts of the design, or use a mixture of bright flowers and seedheads.

A summer horseshoe of sweet peas, roses and spray carnations. The contrasting materials are wispy sprays of golden rod, clusters of small variegated ivy, and scented pelargonium leaves. (LEFT)

Fresh flowers in concentric circles are cleverly held in position by the round wire cooling rack underneath. (LEFT)

33

*S*HAPES FOR AWKWARD SPACES

The wonderful versatility of floral forms makes unused areas ideal for flower arrangements.

There are all kinds of locations around the home where you may want to place a flower arrangement but you are prevented from doing so by lack of space or by the proportions of a room or furniture.

However, there are a number of ways to create eye-catching flower arrangements that fit perfectly into these locations, without looking out of proportion. One way is to compose a flower arrangement as part of a still-life group, using more than one container or placing accessories beside the principal one, so that the eye is carried out to the sides rather than upwards. You may have a collection of mugs or small containers, decorative jars or pots which you could arrange in such a group, adding a few blooms to each mug.

Alternatively, you can arrange flowers of different types but of harmonizing colours in each of the containers.

SPREADING OUT

Another way to spread the focal interest in an arrangement is to place accessories beside it. If you have a pair of matching or complementary plates and dishes, you can use them to double the visual size and impact of the flower design. For example, arrange a low triangle of freesias, roses and spray carnations in one of the plates. Arrange some fresh fruit, cut in half or still whole, in the other plate and the overall design takes on a much wider perspective.

You can use large, shallow containers of all kinds to create beautiful, showy arrangements to display on a sideboard, dining table or shelf. Such an arrangement is shown on the pine bookshelf. Whether the container is dish-shaped or flat, it can make a perfect foundation for a low-level design with style. This type of

A perfect example of working within a confined space. A low-lying triangle of flowers and foliage sits neatly on a pine bookshelf. (BELOW)

arrangement is shown in the shallow white dish containing yellow lilies, daisy chrysanthemums, purple irises and assorted foliage placed on a bookshelf.

Examples of suitable dish-shaped containers for low-profile arrangements include pottery serving dishes, baking dishes, wooden salad bowls and shallow baskets. For a flat container, you can choose from cane, brass and decorative trays, wooden boards and serving dishes.

You can compose low-level displays in a variety of ways, once the holding material is in place. As an example of a design in a dish-shaped container, we chose an ornamental white pottery dish shaped like a shell. A foam-holding saucer is fixed close to the rim in the foreground. The short stems of white daisy chrysanthemums and geranium leaves are pressed close against the foam to conceal the mechanics. A few alstroemeria flowers are positioned to face forwards and the remaining blooms, including golden rosebuds, spray out in a low horizontal shape, just reaching over the far rim of the container. The challenge for the arranger is to work within the confines of the shell shape, using it to frame the flowers and to determine the size of the display.

USING POTPOURRI

This excellent alternative to arranging fresh flowers on a dish is ideal if you want to brighten up a gloomy corner during the winter months. Take a long, narrow basket – preferably one without a handle, so a bread basket is ideal – and fill it with a combination of whole dried flower heads and sweet-smelling potpourri. Try to choose potpourri that suits your colour scheme. Either go for golds, rusts and browns, or opt for reds and pastel pinks perhaps combined with blues and lilacs. This is a particularly pleasant way to cheer up the windowsill in a bathroom or a dark spot in a hallway.

FLORAL RIBBONS

Often floral swags are displayed on a wall, but they have just the size, shape and proportion needed to decorate narrow shelves and mantelpieces, long, low coffee tables and narrow, rectangular dining tables. They also have maximum impact with minimum height – a combination that makes them a perfect choice for low-ceilinged rooms.

All you need as the container is a long, shallow holder, just deep enough to take a 7.5cm (3in) slice cut from a block of florist's foam and just large enough to allow you space, when using fresh flowers, to top up the water. For a floral ribbon, such as the one featured, we used two plastic holders placed end to end and stuck together with a few dabs of florist's adhesive clay. There is no problem with concealing the holding material in a

A handful of short-stemmed flowers, two rectangular plastic holders and florist's foam make up a bright low-lying floral 'ribbon', ideal for a shelf or mantelpiece. (ABOVE)

design of this kind, since almost all the flower stems are cut short and pressed close against the foam. Long stems of freesia and obedient plant (*Physostegia virginiana*) cover the handles, and yellow and white chrysanthemums, pink spray carnations, sprays of rowanberries and individual scented pelargonium leaves make a patchwork of shape and colour that covers the foam and completes the arrangement. To avoid an appearance that is too flat, pink and yellow alstroemeria are added above the 'ground cover' materials, with flowers facing in opposite directions for added texture.

TURNED UPSIDE-DOWN

A novel approach to filling low spaces is to take a glass goldfish bowl or elongated, rectangular vase, carefully fill it to the brim with water and place flowers and foliage upside-down in it. The result will be a mesh of leaves and petals that sparkles like diamonds wherever the air bubbles cling. The flowers are magnified when seen through the water and their colours intensified by the refraction of light. You will create a more dramatic effect if you can position your arrangement near a lamp, or near a window that gets good sunlight through it for most of the day. If you put it in a dark corner, you will diminish the effect you achieve.

As you push the flowers underwater, they will inevitably try to float to the top. The trick for success is to gently trap some of them in the mesh of the foliage, and to wedge some of the stems under the rim of the container. With practice, you will find this becomes easier to do. The end results, in any case will make any initial effort worthwhile as people will always be impressed by such an original flower arrangement.

A pottery dish in an attractive shell shape defines the size and scale of this display of alstroemeria, roses and daisy chrysanthemums. (RIGHT)

SMALL ARRANGEMENTS

Mix delicate leaves and flowers in tiny containers, to prove that small is beautiful.

Sometimes less is more, and the saying is true when you design a miniature display. With large arrangements, you usually work to a preconceived, completed image. With miniature displays, you have less material to work with but you also have much more freedom to improvise and be creative, especially if you are producing several miniatures.

Miniature flower designs are highly compelling. They may not share the drama and impact of large-scale displays but they have a special charm of their own. Their diminutive size requires close attention to fully appreciate the beauty of every tiny leaf and flower. The curve of an anemone stem, for example, may get lost in a large display, but can be the main feature in a miniature. For greater impact, group together a selection of miniature arrangements; sometimes a lone display can look a little lost.

FOLLOWING THE RULES

In floral art clubs and flower arranging competitions, the term 'miniature' does not just mean small. Various governing bodies have established rules and requirements. For example, the National Association of Flower Arrangement Societies (NAFAS), a miniature design should be no more than 10cm (4in) overall. There is ample scope for pleasing and varied designs within this imposed size limit, but of course it is only necessary to adhere strictly to such limits if you plan to enter your flower designs in competitions or exhibitions.

TINY CONTAINERS

Thinking small in terms of flower arrangements means looking around the home for unlikely containers that might double as flower vases, for example, a thimble. To use a thimble as a minute vase, partly fill

Three small coffee cups hold yellow ranunculus cut short and are teamed with dainty violets to achieve a miniature massed-flower look. (BELOW LEFT)

A handful of strawberry flowers, a few buttercups and a pink hydrangea head make an artistic floral composition using the minimum of materials. (BELOW RIGHT)

An elegant corsage of freesias and nerines. Each flower and leaf in the design is separately wired. Spray it with water and put it in a box at the bottom of the refrigerator to keep fresh overnight. (ABOVE)

little snippings of shiny white sea lavender, minute purple and yellow wild violas and a couple of buttercups will attract more attention when placed on a golden or silver coin. A plain brown bottle cap with a cascade of lime-green lady's mantle, a few trails of lobelia and short-cut stems of quaking grass looks even more rustic when displayed on a suitably sized wooden base. For a more modern composition, fill a bright red bottle cap with a fiery selection of red and yellow flowers and a few sprays of red begonia leaves or red-stemmed herb Robert.

OUT OF THE ORDINARY
Small shells make romantic containers. Use those that have a deep enough aperture to hold a piece of soaked foam. Very few shells are cavernous and steady enough on their sides to be filled with water safely.

Bi-valve shells, those composed of two hinged sections, look delightful with flowers and foliage arranged to spill out of the aperture, cornucopia-style. Just conceal a fragment of florist's foam between the two halves to water the flowers. Even grey mussel shells which can simply be picked up off a beach, look effective displayed like this, and a group of them arranged on a flat plate makes an unusual and attractive design for a dining table or a low coffee or occasional table.

MINIATURE BOXES
Boxes of all kinds make charming containers for small-scale designs and can be used in a similar way to bi-valve shells. Snuff boxes, pillboxes, heart-shaped trinket boxes and brightly coloured miniature painted tin boxes make lovely little flower containers. Waterproof wooden boxes to ensure they are not damaged prior to inserting wet foam.

Miniature boxes call for arrangements of dainty, romantic flowers. To outline the height and width of the design, use green material, such as chive leaves, thin sprigs of thyme, sturdy blades of grass, the tips of broom, rosemary and yew shoots, cypress or juniper clippings. Silver-grey possibilities include thin sprays of lavender, pink, carnation, curry plant and artemisia leaves. Use small compact flowers to fill the centre of the display, such as pale pink thrift, mauve chive flowers, scarlet pimpernel and yellow senecio.

it with water for a doll's house-sized bunch of flowers but be sure to check that the base is level or it will topple over. Some are domed on top and even a thimble-full of water can spoil the surface of a favourite piece of furniture.

Other extra-small containers include caps of drinks bottles. One brand of whisky has a particularly attractive golden cap that makes a perfectly-shaped vase when turned upside down. Caps of spice jars, perfume bottles and sauce bottles all have possibilities. Before you throw them away, check that they can't be saved for use as an unusual miniature vase.

HOLDING SMALL FLOWERS
Before inserting a tiny piece of soaked foam into a small container, check whether the flower stems are strong enough to be pushed into damp foam without breaking. Those with reasonably firm stems, such as buttercups, crane's bill, lady's mantle or gypsophila, should be suitable. Flowers with tender stems need more careful treatment. Ease their way into the foam by making a hole first, using a wooden cocktail stick.

A golden drinks-bottle cap filled with

USING LARGE MATERIAL

It may seem surprising, but some of the most effective materials to use in small scale designs are larger plants. Look around the garden for likely candidates to supply suitable material. Side shoots of towering plants, such as delphinium, larkspur and clarkia, can be snipped into separate elements. In a small design, the tip of a shoot in tight bud and one or two florets will take on an entirely different perspective. Double and single stocks, with their rich, lingering scent can be used in a similar way. Two or three tightly packed pink, yellow, blue, mauve or white stock flowers snipped from the main stem can form the focal point of a miniature.

Use sweet peas in a similar way. A single stem may have seven or eight flowers on stems with intriguing twists and curves – more than enough to fill a design in a pillbox or a triangular design in a ramekin dish.

GROUPED ARRANGEMENTS

Miniature arrangements look highly effective when they are placed together in mixed groups. Use old bottles, small clay jugs and pots, tiny glass vases or wicker-covered bottles. Choose flowers of a single colour to unify the displays. For example, use only white flowers and silver foliage, pansies, gypsophila, miniature roses, tight rose buds, heather, feverfew or marguerites together with sprays of ballota, sage, campion or variegated mints.

Alternatively, create a kaleidoscope effect by arranging each container with a different flower type and a different colour. A tall glass bottle could hold a single mauve teasel flower; a wicker basket, a nosegay of buttercups and daises; and a slender glass vase, a trio of mauve, orange and yellow pansies.

DISPLAYING MINIATURES

Small-scale arrangements need careful positioning to appreciate fully their delicate beauty. Display them singly or in groups on a dressing table, bedside table or bathroom shelf. Brighten up kitchen nooks and crannies with a collection of mini-stoneware containers filled with tiny flowers or line an empty windowsill with a row of low-lying flowers in a mixture of colours. Wrap fresh flowers in a doily collar. The paper surround acts as a

frame, so each tiny flower and leaf spray can be appreciated individually. Select a doily that is in scale with your design – too large and it will swamp the flowers. Fold the doily in half and half again, snip the point and push the flower stems through the hole. Pleat the doily around the bunch and bind the stems with stub wire and green tape.

A small yellow and white bunch set on top of a blue medicine bottle, a romantic pink or cream one resting in a small shallow basket – these make miniature designs with an enchanting difference.

PLACING MINIATURES

Miniature displays are easily over-looked and knocked over, so take extra care in finding a suitable setting. Wall-hung, open-fronted display cabinets are excellent, providing the flowers and foliage don't project too far beyond the front face. You can sometimes buy old-fashioned wooden typesetters' boxes, to hang on the wall; or use narrow glass shelves, such as those in a modern medicine cabinet.

Although the displays need to be safe, they need to be close enough for you to appreciate the beauty of flowers.

Tiny sprigs of flowers contrast with foliage, seedheads and sprays of herbs to produce a delicate display. They are given a Victorian look with a frame made from a paper doily. (ABOVE)

STEP *by* STEP

Small Arrangement

Miniature displays are especially easy to create if you have a garden, as you can pick just the flowers you want, and as few as you like, together with little bits of foliage. Florists sell mixed bunches, often including small carnations and rose buds, which can provide material for several miniature arrangements. In spring, grape hyacinths, primroses and violets are perfect for miniature displays with a few sprigs of houseplant cuttings or garden foliage added.

When you shape florist's foam to fit larger arrangements, save the off-cuts for miniatures. Corners, strips and thin slices of foam will come in handy when you want to arrange flowers in small containers, such as a pillbox thimble or cup and saucer.

Miniature displays are ideal for giving a second lease of life to cut flowers which are beginning to look past their best. When you take apart a tired arrangement, shorten the stems of those flowers that are still attractive enough to be used as the basis for new miniature displays.

Small garden flowers – bleeding heart, lilac blossom, forget-me-not, wallflower, roses and gypsophila – are chosen to harmonize with the hues, delicate style and proportion of this china bowl. (RIGHT)

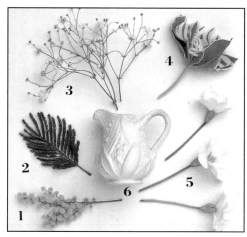

YOU WILL NEED

1 *4 sprigs of mimosa flowers*
2 *3 sprigs of mimosa foliage*
3 *3 sprays of white gypsophila*
4 *2 sprigs of euphorbia*
5 *5 cream polyanthus flowers*
6 *small white milk jug*

1

2

3

4

1 Fill the milk jug with water. Trim the stems of variegated euphorbia to 8-10cm (3-4in). Place them in the jug, letting them fall naturally to the rim to form a cool green background.

2 Trim the stems of mimosa flowers to 10cm (4in). Place them in the vase so they arch to the left, right and centre of the jug. Add the foliage of the same length towards the outside.

3 Add the 13cm (5in) sprays of white gypsophila right around the other flowers to fill any gaps in the display and give a hazy outline to the overall shape.

4 Condition the polyanthus. Insert them in the centre of the display where their golden centres will be highlighted by the nearby mimosa flowers.

*L*ARGE ARRANGEMENTS

Create dramatic focal points in your home with floor-standing seasonal displays on a large scale.

However small the size of a room or closely packed it is with furniture and other furnishings, you can always make space for a ground-level floral design. Display a bright vase with some equally bright blooms in it, or a basket brimming with vivid dahlias or chrysanthemums.

Doorways are the obvious place to start when thinking of where to position floor-standing displays. Position one or two pots of pink, blue or red hydrangeas to create a welcoming impression. The huge mop-headed flowers give a long showing of colour and, just before they fade, you can cut them off and air dry them for more permanent displays.

Garden centres sell a huge selection of containers to suit large arrangements. You can buy stoneware look-alike ones, some of which are made of lightweight plastic. Terracotta pots, some rough textured and decorated with rope-ware or medallion designs, others smooth and plain, also look good positioned on either side of a doorway. Where space is limited, look for narrow containers, such as old-fashioned chimney pots, available from bric-a-brac stalls and junk and second-hand shops.

CONTAINER SIZES

The actual size of the container does not necessarily determine the scale of an arrangement. A large urn-shaped pot can hold many types of flowers.

A crescent-shaped cascade of foliage and flowers, trailing from side to side of the urn and forming a hummocky dome across the top is just as effective for a floor-standing arrangement. This froth-of-flowers look is especially suitable for displays to stand in a hallway or at the bend of the stairs, where they will be viewed from above.

To achieve this dripping-with-colour look in a deep container, stand a platform inside — one or two plastic tubs or boxes

would do — and a tray of soaked foam on top. Trail stems of clematis or honeysuckle over the sides, form the mound shapes with short-cut clusters of Michaelmas daises and use a handful of *Rudbeckia purpurea* to provide the highlights.

CORNER INTEREST

Once past the threshold, room corners can be the next focus of attention for floor-standing floral designs. There may be space for a large tub or wooden-box container of climbing plants trained up vertical canes.

A more decorative alternative is to use a standard lamp or a coat-rack as the climbing frame, with a tub or two of foliage planted at its feet.

ROOM DIVIDERS

Painted and decorated wooden boxes on legs can be used as room dividers to give one end of a large open-plan living area a more intimate feel. You can adapt a window box for the purpose. Fill the trough with suitable mixed flowering and foliage plants. Use ordinary glass jars to hold the flowers as they won't be seen, but make sure you arrange the plant material to conceal them. Take the colour cue from your furnishings — a profusion of mauve and shocking pink asters will intensify the colours in a pale pink or blue room, and a cheerful display of orange and red dahlias will enliven pale yellow or create a splash against white.

Look out for troughs in antique shops. Polish them up with beeswax to restore a glossy shine and they will make unusual room dividers. You will need to raise the base level of the trough in order to display a cut-flower arrangement — a plank of wood resting on two pillars of bricks inside the trough will do the trick. A large bushy arrangement of brown-flecked, pink and tawny alstroemeria would look spectacular in such a setting. Use a

*L*arge displays cannot help but create a dramatic focal point in your home, particularly if you use flowers like these stunning anthuriums. (*FAR RIGHT*)

A display of fruit and flowers in a basket that makes the most of a handful of produce. The basket base is packed with newspaper and a small block of florist's foam. (RIGHT)

number of wide-mouthed containers fitted with chicken wire to support an airy mass of flowers and give the illusion that they are standing directly in the trough.

UNUSUAL CONTAINERS

Some unusual containers that would be too cumbersome on tables or at eye level are ideal for floor-standing arrangements. You may have some around the home already but never thought of putting flowers in them. Position a single vibrant gerbera in the spout of a terracotta

drinking vessel. Pack out a tall pottery umbrella stand with dramatic, chocolate-brown bulrushes, or choose tall, feathery pampas grass for a more delicate effect.

Old cider crocks make decorative floor-level containers for indoor or outdoor displays and look particularly good filled with the muted tones of hydrangea heads, which balance their bulk. A modern glass demijohn designed for home wine production is another alternative. The clarity and freshness of green glass demands purity and lightness from flowers – a few delicate

Brighten a doorway or porch with a vibrant display – a handful of yellow daisies and contrasting purple statice arranged informally in a pink enamel jug. (LEFT)

gypsophila stems (trimmed of leaves) blossoming in a frothy cloud of the confetti-like blooms would be perfect.

Another eye-catching idea is to place a wide shallow bowl of water on a wooden floor and float vibrantly coloured flower-heads in it. But always make sure to place it somewhere where it will not be kicked over. Choose a fruit or salad bowl with a brightly painted interior, or a bowl from a Victorian washbasin set and float in it a single full-blown rose to waft a delicate perfume in the bedroom.

THINKING BIG

For dramatic floorshows of flowers you need to think big. For a late-summer evening party, create a glow of colour that will intensify as the light fades with a big display of hot pink and yellow antir-rhinums in an enamel laundry bowl or an old ceramic sink. A two-tiered arrange-ment in an old-fashioned hip bath would be best of all. They often come in faded blues and greens, which would combine well with scabious, love-in-a-mist, laven-der and sea holly.

STEP *by* STEP

Large Arrangements

Use a flower-filled urn display to transform your room into an indoor garden — especially useful if you're entertaining and the conservatory or sun room plants aren't quite in flower yet. The urn, with its classical overtones, demands a spacious, formal setting. A large entrance hall, living room or dining room would be ideal. If you're having an afternoon or evening garden party and the weather's fine, move the whole display on to the patio for an elegant, welcoming touch.

CHOOSING THE CONTAINER

The cost of a genuine antique stone urn is prohibitive, but you can buy attractive, reasonably-priced concrete urns, in a range of styles and sizes, at larger garden centres. Some are cast in moulds taken of antique urns and look authentic, but would need to be waterproofed for use in a fresh flower display.

The urn that is used in our featured display is made of fibreglass, and is much cheaper and more lightweight than a concrete urn. There are several ways to camouflage such urns and make them appear more solid. If you use the urn frequently for flower displays, it's worth taking a bit more trouble to camouflage the plastic.

Use an emulsion paint, in grey-green, mid-grey, creamy-beige or other stone-like colour. For the urn featured here, a small tin of emulsion is used. Add enough coarse sand to give the paint texture and stir thoroughly. Make sure the urn is clean and dry and prime the surface with an undercoat. When dry use a medium-sized paintbrush and stipple the urn with the paint and sand mixture.

Divide the remaining paint in half. Add a little black paint to one half and, with a

Gorgeous flowers abound in a Grecian-style urn that is sure to be an immediate focus of attention, no matter where you place it. (FAR RIGHT)

WIRING GERBERAS

Gerbera stems tend to bend and droop when put on display. To keep them straight and in the required position you can provide artificial support for the flowerheads by reinforcing the stems with wire.

Take a 20cm (8in) length of stub wire and bind it along its length with green gutta percha tape to prevent the stub wire from rusting and to help camouflage the wire.

Starting at the top of the flower stem just below the flowerhead, wrap the wire once around the top of the stem and work your way down, twisting the remainder of the wire around the stem as you go. The wire does not have to reach to the bottom as long as it provides support for the flowerhead and most of the stem.

smaller brush, paint over any indentations in the urn, to define them and make them appear to recede. Mix the remaining paint with a little white and use it to highlight the raised parts of the urn surface. Keep the brush strokes rough and irregular to simulate the surface of stone.

PICKING YOUR FLOWERS

This arrangement is based on creamy peach, pale yellow, pink and white. A mixture of pink and yellow alstroemeria establishes the basic colour scheme. They are reasonably priced at the florist, but

day lilies from the garden could be used as an alternative.

Gerberas, like alstroemeria, are available throughout the year and are ideal for this display, but you could always substitute garden paeonies or tulips, if you prefer.

The Madonna lily, with its fragrant white flowers, can be expensive so you could use cheaper oriental lilies instead. Similarly, the arching sprays of white and yellow-flowered broom cascading over the rim of the urn could be swapped with sprays of bear grass.

CREATING A FLOWER-FILLED URN

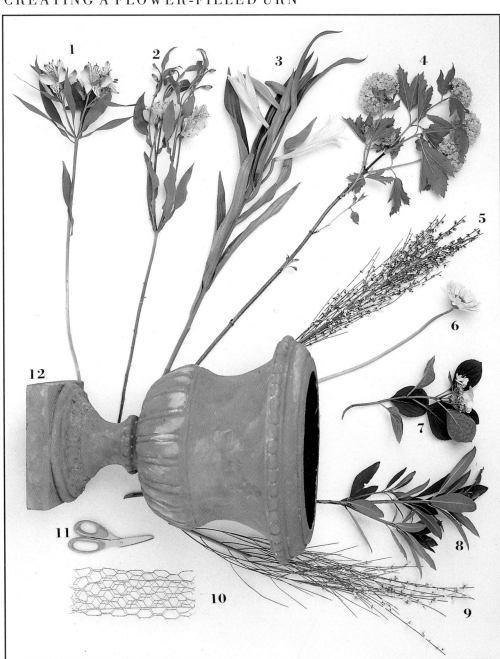

YOU WILL NEED

1 5 stems of pink alstroemeria
2 5 stems of lemon-yellow alstroemeria
3 3 stems of Madonna lilies
4 2 stems of Viburnum opulus 'Sterile'
5 1 bunch of white broom
6 5 stems of pink gerberas
7 5 stems of hydrangea
8 3 stems of rhododendron foliage
9 1 bunch of lemon-yellow broom
10 1m (3ft) of chicken wire
11 floristry scissors
12 stone or fibreglass urn

1

2

3

4

5

6

1 Mould 1m (3ft) of chicken wire into a cylinder shape to fit into the mouth of the urn. Bend over the top of the wire so that it joins together to form a dome shape to support the flowers. Press the chicken wire in place in the urn. Fill the urn two-thirds full of water.

2 Use three rhododendron branches to set the height of the arrangement. The stems should be about one and a half times the height of the urn. Place two rhododendron stems upright at the back of the display. Position the third stem in the middle right of the display.

3 Trim one stem of *Viburnum opulus* 'Sterile' so that it is similar in height to the tallest rhododendron stem. Cut the second stem about 20cm (8in) shorter. At the bottom of each stem make a small, vertical snip to help the woody stems take up water. Place both branches in the centre of the display.

4 Take five stems of both lemon and pink alstroemeria and remove any leaves at the bottom of the stem ends. Trim off about 5cm (2in) at an angle from each stem end. Arrange each stem in turn, across the front of the urn.

5 Take three or four broom stems in your hand and gently ease them into curves. Add broom in mixed-colour groups of three or four stems. Position the broom stems at the front of the arrangement, so that they cascade over the rim of the urn, disguising its rigid line.

6 Strip the lower leaves from three Madonna lily stems then place them towards the centre back of the urn. Next arrange five hydrangea stems to form a collar around the urn rim. Insert the gerberas last and position them in the centre

Containers

RESOURCEFUL FLOWER ARRANGERS NEVER RUN OUT OF
CONTAINERS. EVEN THE MOST UNLIKELY-LOOKING HOUSEHOLD
OBJECTS HAVE POTENTIAL AND CAN BE TRANSFORMED INTO
ATTRACTIVE – IF UNUSUAL – FLOWER HOLDERS.

Putting on the style with mahonia leaves, freesia and clusters of wired-on fruits cascading from a scooped-out pineapple shell. (RIGHT)

At those times when all your usual vases are in use or you simply feel like something different, it's fun to explore the possibilities of all kinds of articles around the home that can be used to hold an arrangement of flowers. There's hidden potential in even the most basic kitchen equipment, and all it takes is a little imagination to turn everyday implements into attractive containers.

To hold fresh flowers, a container simply needs to be able to conceal a small holder of water – and the water-carrier can be as slender and unobtrusive as an orchid phial or a piece of soaked stem-holding foam.

The improvised container does not even have to have an opening, as several of the colour photographs demonstrate. The foam (suitably covered, to avoid moisture seepage) can be fixed on top of a box, to a basket handle, on to a figurine or other ornament, and then completely concealed by judiciously placed leaves and short-stemmed flowers.

NEW APPROACHES

The hunt for containers with a difference begins at home – though junk shops, car boot sales, garden centres and supermarkets all have valuable and inexpensive contributions to make.

Tableware of all kinds makes perfect flower holders. Cups and saucers, with a bunch of flowers in the cup and a single tiny flower floating in the saucer; tea and coffee pots, jugs in all shapes and sizes, from the romantically flowery to angular modern styles, offer inspiration for the colour and shape of your various different flower designs.

Saucers and plates make flat and spacious, versatile flower holders. All they need is a block of foam held firmly in place to secure flowers in triangular, L-shaped or random designs.

DIFFERENT MATERIALS

Elegant china containers are probably best suited to formal designs outlined with slender leaves. Ceramic containers have their own particular appeal. From the palest pastels to bright primary colours and earthy terracotta, a ceramic container can be chosen to emphasize or contrast with the colour of the flowers. As ceramic vases are opaque, different styles can be achieved by using stem-holding material to keep flowers in place.

A child's wooden train makes an unusual and stylish container for a bright selection of flowers. (FAR RIGHT)

Create an impressive buffet table display using hollowed-out red, green and yellow peppers as containers. (ABOVE)

Metal containers have varying effects on the mood of an arrangement. Cold-looking metals, such as pewter, make the flower colour seem cool, whereas yellow metals, like brass and copper, lend a warm glow to flowers.

KITCHEN CLASSICS
Saucepans, casseroles, lemon squeezers and storage jars – all of these items and any others with an aperture deep or spacious enough to hold water or conceal a piece of foam can be used for displays.

If you have a metal vegetable or herb mill that is only in occasional use, it could become the centre of attention at your next informal party. Line the bowl of the vessel with foil (since it isn't watertight) and wedge in a block of soaked foam to extend above the rim. The kitchen has all kinds of flat containers to offer: shiny-bright baking pans, cake tins, confectionery moulds, wire cooling racks – the list is enormous.

Take, for example, a black four-hole Yorkshire pudding pan. Attach a block of foam to one of the indentations, top up with water and style an arrangement of brightly coloured flowers, leaves or berries that will be vividly displayed against the dense, matt surface.

To make use of a flat container that has no convenient indentation, wedge the foam into an unobtrusive container of its own – an up-turned coffee jar lid is ideal –

and tape it to the (absolutely dry) surface, using florist's tape.

NOVEL CONTAINERS
Much modern packaging has great style, so don't overlook the potential value of old food, drink and cosmetic containers; tins, jars, bottles and packets as unusual, yet striking flower containers. A collection of cola cans turned flower containers would be eye-catching and appropriate in the centre of a teenage party table; stylish cosmetic jars are at home with a bunch of tiny flowers on a dressing-table; and wine bottles make tall and practical 'vases' for long-stemmed material such as hippeastrum or alstroemeria.

Food packets as flower containers are not as impractical as they might seem. Partly fill them with dried beans or tiny pebbles as ballast to ensure the arrangement doesn't topple over, line the top with a double layer of foil and insert a piece of soaked foam. After that, use them as normal containers.

Practically any foodstuff that has a firm outer shell or can be hollowed out to leave firm, sturdy walls, will hold flowers.

A cottage loaf is a splendid example of such an unconventional container. Scrape out the centre and put the shell in a cool oven to dry thoroughly (the bread shell will keep, in a dry place, for weeks). For an extra-shiny finish, paint the crust with clear varnish.

Insert a waterproof container (if using fresh flowers) into the loaf cavity. Fill it with water or wedge it in with soaked foam and treat it as any other flower container.

SCOOP OUT YOUR FRUIT
Pineapples and pumpkins, melons, marrows and citrus fruits of all kinds can be treated in a similar way. Cut a slice from the top, scoop out the flesh and wash and dry the shell. Check that it will stand firm, and cut a slice from the base if necessary. It is possible to dry out pineapple shells in the oven, but other fruit shells tend to crack, wither and otherwise lose their natural sparkle, so its best to regard these as only short-term flower holders.

Line the fruit or vegetable shells with a layer of kitchen plastic wrap if you wish and insert a container for the water or foam. A pineapple fitted with a high-rise block of foam looks good enough to eat

This hollowed-out (and oven-dried) cottage loaf makes a crisp and shiny container for sprays of eucalyptus and gerberas, spray chrysanthemums and a carnation in marmalade hues. (LEFT)

spilling over with a cascade of lesser fruits and brilliant flowers; orange shells lined with egg cups make neat little vases for sprigs of violets, forget-me-nots, snowdrops and other miniature flowers; a dark green melon shell would look dramatic with russetty leaves and glowing berries.

MORE UNUSUAL CONTAINERS

Children's toys, a wooden truck or bus, a small dolls' pram or cradle, can be just the shape to inspire a floral creation – big,

bold and beautiful for a bus, dainty and feminine for a cradle. And out-grown, leather-look boots, polished till they gleam, look just the thing in a corner, resplendent in the autumn months festooned with an elaborate array of twigs and seedheads.

Many old family favourite articles that are broken or no longer in use do not need to be discarded. Items as unlikely as electrical gadgets such as cameras and radios make surprisingly attractive, unique containers for flowers.

BASKETS AS CONTAINERS

Baskets make versatile and indispensable containers for a whole variety of arrangements.

Baskets are infinitely adaptable. You can use them to create any style of arrangement, from a casual country-look composition of trailing stems and shaggy foliage to a neat floral display for a special dinner party.

Available in a huge range of shapes and sizes, there are baskets to suit any type of arrangement. They are woven from a variety of materials, either natural stems or man-made fibres, in an assortment of colours. This makes them almost indispensable to the keen arranger looking for new and inexpensive containers.

NEW POSSIBILITIES

Not all baskets, of course, are designed to hold flowers. Much of the fun of using them as containers comes from discovering possibilities in those intended for far more practical purposes. Wastepaper baskets, cutlery trays, linen baskets, garden trugs, shopping baskets and picnic hampers can all be transformed into original containers to suit a range of flower designs.

Wastepaper baskets, whether they are woven in willow or shaped from spirals of plaited rushes, are large enough to hold a floor-standing display for a fireplace, passage, room corner or porch.

FILLING DEEP BASKETS

Deep basket containers such as wastepaper baskets, look good with long-stemmed fresh material. Indeed, if you want to arrange a bunch of forsythia or laburnum branches, leafy foliage or fruit blossom, a wastepaper basket may be the only container you have that is deep enough to hold it.

After weighting the base of the basket with some clean stones or bricks, fill it with crumpled newspaper. Then you will need to fit the basket with some kind of stem-holding apparatus before you can start arranging. If the stems are long enough to reach to the base of the basket and still look in proportion, you need only stand a bucket in the basket, fix a ball of crumpled wire netting in the neck and tie it firmly to the rim.

The other way – more suitable for shorter stems – is to stand a platform (such as an upturned bowl) in the basket and position a shallow bowl on that. Stand one or two blocks of pre-soaked foam in the dish and tie them in place. Remember to keep the foam moist.

LOW-LYING FLOWERS

Woven cutlery trays make interesting containers for displays of a completely different style. Their flat shapes make them ideal for low-lying, table-top designs. There is no need to fill the whole of the tray or basket with flowers, however. If you use a large, flat container with

Spray-painted pastel blue and pink, the basket suggests the tonal theme for a summer garden selection including phlox, geranium mallow, stock, scabious and scented pelargonium leaves. (RIGHT)

plenty of textural interest, you can give impact to a relatively small amount of material.

One unusual way to turn a cutlery tray into a flower container is to place a few herb and spice jars around the divisions. If the surface of the basket is not quite level, steady the jars with a blob of blue tacky clay underneath each one. Make up small bunches of unruly stems and tiny wild flowers for each jar. For a different look, you could conceal a cylinder of foam in a plastic tub at one end of a cutlery basket and create a triangular arrangement that curves forwards. A design made up of grasses and cereals, marguerites and poppies would be in perfect harmony with a bleached willow container.

Rustic baskets filled with flowers or fruit and flowers bring country charms into your home. (ABOVE)

FLOWERS IN SHOPPING BASKETS

Narrow-woven shopping baskets of the grip-handle or shoulder-bag type provide a wealth of possibilities for wonderful flower designs.

You can hang one on the back of a door or in a hallway and arrange a sheaf of flowers to spill out over one edge. If you want a more permanent display, use dried flowers. Fluffy, lacy shapes like pale pink silene, silvery acacia and green chenopodium seedheads suit this shape well. If you prefer you could opt for a more symmetrical shape and arrange a fanburst of flowers to come out over the rim of the basket.

To arrange fresh flowers in a shoulder basket you simply have to conceal inside it a block of soaked foam set into a plastic box or tub. Position the foam so that it extends a little above the rim. This enables you to angle and slant stems sideways and downwards. Yellow spray chrysanthemums alternating with warm russet wallflowers and cool cream freesias make a lovely combination for a design that would look equally at home hanging alongside a fireplace, on a balcony, or in your hallway or kitchen.

WEAVING A DESIGN

Whether they are woven of natural willow, craggy vine twigs, hazel or mountain ash stems, reeds, rushes or bamboo, most baskets are fine examples of craftsmanship. If you find one that is old and worn or just too plain to be used as an attractive container for flowers you can decorate it.

If you have a basket with widely spaced vertical slats, a very open weave or a gap in the weave pattern, you can thread fresh or dried stems in and out to add texture

A large shopping basket doubles as an outdoor flower container. There is plenty of depth for a bowl and a block of foam to hold the cascade of chrysanthemums, wallflowers, freesias and bear grass. (RIGHT)

A mouth-watering display of fruit one side and a mass of carnations, green orchids and freesias on the other add up to a party design perfect for a buffet table or sideboard. (LEFT)

and colour. The basket uprights will hold the stems firmly in place. Simply thread one after another, slightly overlapping the stems where they join. You do not have to make any special fastenings.

Rosemary stems will make a thick green basket wall and retain their re-freshing fragrance as they dry; thyme stems give a woody and straggly appear-ance and santolina stems stay a pretty, silvery-grey colour as they dry. All will contrast well with dark-brown basket weaves. Lavender stems can be woven four or five at a time to make a sweet-scented basket that will look lovely with a casual arrangement of roses.

Decorate a broad-rimmed basket by sticking flowerheads all along it. Helichrysum flowers are particularly suit-able and give a bright and colourful ribbon effect.

DECORATING THE HANDLE

Much of the charm and character of some baskets is in the shape of the handle, whether it is a tall hoop or a pair of small hand-grips at the sides. Emphasize the elegant curve of a handle by following the line with arched stems such as broom, artemesia and ivy.

To incorporate a high handle into your flower design, you can bind it with an evergreen such as ivy or wire on a small block of pre-soaked foam wrapped in foil. This provides a source of water for trails of leaves and flowers to arch around the curve of the handle. Conceal the foam with closely-arranged, short-stemmed flowers. Place them tightly together so they hide as much of the foam as possible.

STEP *by* STEP

Flower Basket

Basket displays are always a popular choice for keen flower arrangers. On many occasions though the flowers shown are dried and require a 'dried technique' of arranging. This arrangement makes a welcome change by explaining just how to create a fabulous basket arrangement of fresh flowers in a moss-covered basket.

DESIGN STRATEGY

In most conventional flower displays, the flowers and foliage are loosely arranged, so that there are empty spaces within the display, and the flowers and foliage occupy an area larger than their own bulk. These pockets of 'internal' space are important in terms of design, as they create a feeling of airiness and allow the shape of each flower to be appreciated to the fullest.

One of the joys of flower arranging, however, is the wealth of different approaches that can be taken, with equally attractive end results. The flowers in this display are an example of another set of principles. The flowers are arranged in a condensed layer, so that all the air space is excluded, and one mass of

SIZING UP FLORIST'S FOAM

A florist's foam block, whether for fresh or dried flowers, can hold many times its own height and width in flowers. There's no need to fill a basket completely with florist's foam; it is wasteful, makes the arrangement very difficult to water, and in the case of large, fresh displays, very heavy. Unless you're using florist's adhesive clay and prongs, though, the foam block must be wedged securely in the basket.

flowers fits tightly against another.

Though the effect is one of sophisticated richness, it is really a simple arrangement to make, as the shape of the basket dictates the build-up of flowers. Since all the flowers and foliage are cut to much the same length, you don't have to worry about varying heights. Make sure, however, that some groups of flowers are slightly larger than others, or the end result is liable to be somewhat bland and uninteresting.

PLANNING AHEAD

When composing a design — however formal or informal — in which the shape of the plant material plays an important role, making a sketched plan of it first may help you to visualize a successful display. Draw in the outline shape of the container you plan to use, and then add the shape and proportions of the principal flowers. Obviously, if you work with coloured pens or pencils you will be able to work on your colour scheme at the same time. Once you have seen your plan on paper, it will be easier to select the most appropriate plant materials, position them correctly and thus provide a framework for the other flowers.

THE BASIC IDEA

The display is a study in contrasting textures and shapes. The huge, trumpet-shaped hippeastrums contrast effectively with the smaller, rounded, tightly-packed chrysanthemum heads and the papery, lacy statice. The alstroemeria and nerines repeat the trumpet theme, but on a more delicate scale.

It is a warm-toned arrangement, made up of a subtle combination of pink, peach, coral, scarlet and vibrant orange flowers. An alternative would be to concentrate on whites and creams — all of the featured flowers are also available in these colours

– or you could make it tonally stronger, including richer oranges, mahoganies and crimsons. Even changing the hippeastrum from apple-blossom pink, as shown, to scarlet, would make a dramatic difference to the effect.

A word of warning: although white would 'go' with the colours shown in this display, a few white flowers would visually jump out at you, and destroy the deliberately smooth, even surface effect of the similar-coloured pink, peach, coral, orange and scarlet.

Though this is a moderately priced, as opposed to a 'cheap and cheerful' display, it is long lasting, and there is one cost-saving you could make. As all the flower stems are cut short before insertion, ask for 'shorts' at the florist shop,

these are cheaper than their long-stemmed counterparts.

CHOOSING THE FLOWERS

Three stems of double-spray chrysanthemums, in a russetty-orange tinged with pink, are used. Double spray chrysanthemums come in a huge range of warm, subtle colours, and you could choose a slightly pinker or slightly browner variety instead. Single spray carnations could also be used, since the individual flowers compact well into a purely textural surface. Their colours tend to be less subtle, though.

Statice, or annual sea lavender, is sold fresh in summer and autumn, and dried, all year round. Fresh or dried statice could be used here, although the stems of

The rich, tapestry-like effect of this pretty, fresh-flower filled basket is best appreciated from above. Display it in pride of place on a coffee table or on a low side-table.
(ABOVE)

MAKING A BASKET WATERPROOF

Some wicker baskets are sold ready-lined with polythene or plastic to make them waterproof, but others aren't. It's easy to convert a porous basket to a waterproof one, just follow the steps below.

Alternatively, slip a disposable aluminium cooking container into the basket and mould it to the required shape – it doesn't have to come all the way up the sides; it should just have enough rim reaching up around the inside of the basket to catch any excess water.

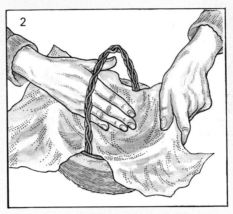

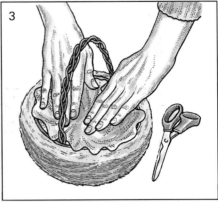

1 Cut off small pieces of florist's adhesive clay and stick little dabs around the inside rim and on the base of the basket.
2 Take a large square of plastic or polythene and place it inside the

basket so you can judge how much to trim.
3 Trim the square to the appropriate size and place it in the basket. Press the plastic down on to the base and against the rim.

dried statice would eventually rot through contact with the damp florist's foam, and would have to be discarded at the end of the display.

The peachy shade used is only just becoming fashionable, and though bunches of peach-coloured statice are starting to appear in shops, you may have to buy several mixed bunches, and extract the peach-coloured flowers from the more usual yellow, purple, white and pink shades. Save these for another display, or ask your florist to order a bunch of peach-coloured statice for you. Fresh statice is also long lasting, up to two weeks if bought when most of the calyces are open and showing colour.

Alstroemeria is another year-round favourite. Its colour range is more limited than chrysanthemums, but it more than

makes up for it by having a seemingly infinite range of contrasting stripes, spots, or bands on the petals. Here, three stems of rich coral-coloured alstroemeria are used, with a deep yellow 'throat' and mahogany-brown lines, which in nature serve to guide insects into the centre of the flowers to pollinate them. Alstroemeria is sold by the bunch or stem. The number of flowers per stem varies from three to seven, so if you can buy it by the stem, go for those with the largest number of flowers and buds. (Choosing stems with buds as well as open flowers means that your display will last that much longer.)

Six to seven stems of orange-scarlet nerine, or Guernsey lily, are also used. One of the paler varieties could be used, but, if you are keeping to the colour scheme shown, avoid varieties with fuchsia-pink flowers. Guernsey lily's prominent, long stamens are one of its most attractive features, protruding well beyond the petals.

HIPPEASTRUM HINTS

Hippeastrum, sometimes confusingly called amaryllis, is the most unusual cut flower in this display, and also the most expensive. Hippeastrum is more often seen as a bulbous house plant; it is sold dormant in autumn for flowering around Christmas or in early spring.

When hippeastrum flowers are used on their full-length stems, it is common floristry practice to stick a cane inside the hollow stem to help support the flowers. Here, the problem of a weak stem is eliminated by cutting it short.

Hippeastrum is also unusual in that the flowers appear before the leaves – also true of nerine, to which it is related. Large oriental-hybrid lilies, such as the popular pink and white 'Stargazer', could be used instead; 'Stargazer' would also provide a welcome fragrance which this display otherwise lacks.

Hippeastrum flowers come in colours ranging from white through pink, salmon-orange and scarlet – here, an apple-blossom pink is used. Hippeastrums should last a week if fresh when bought.

CHOOSING THE FOLIAGE

Two types of evergreen foliage are included: huge, palmate fatsia leaves, and the smaller variegated pittosporum. Fatsia is sometimes sold as a house plant, but its natural home is in the garden, where its tolerance of shade and pollution ensures its popularity as a town-garden plant. Fatsia is sometimes stocked by florists, but it is such a popular plant that you're bound to find a friend or neighbour with a few leaves to spare. You could use, instead, the similar but slightly smaller leaves of *Fatshedera lizei*, a bigeneric hybrid between fatsia and ivy.

There are hardy forms of pittosporum, but *Pittosporum tobira* 'Variegata', the variety used here, is too tender for all but the very mildest localities. Fortunately, it is widely carried by florists, and is available all year round. You could use sprigs of the hardy evergreen *Euonymus japonicus* instead, but avoid the yellow-variegated sorts – these would be too vivid for this delicate-looking display.

CHOOSING THE CONTAINER

In this display, a moss and wicker basket, about 30cm (12 in) across, is used, but most natural wicker baskets could be substituted. Front-facing wicker baskets, with high, built-up backs, are unsuitable for this round-shaped display as are 'Bo-Peep' types, with awkwardly narrow bases and splayed-out sides. Although a handle adds interest to the display, it isn't essential. You could, if you like, make a feature of the handle by winding ribbon in

This arrangement uses tightly-packed flowers to create a rich tonal pattern. The idea would translate beautifully into a creamy-white scheme. (ABOVE)

REMOVING SEPALS

Before arranging nerines, remove their papery sepals. Not only are they unattractive, they use up water that should go towards extending the life of the flower; the same is true of chrysanthemum leaves. And always remove the lowest leaves from a cut stem, otherwise they enlarge the holes in the foam block when the stems are inserted, causing instability. They would also make the water smell foul very quickly.

a complementary shade around it and making a bow.

Ready-mossed baskets are widely available from florists, or you can easily make one up yourself. Moss damages easily, though, so treat the basket with care. Newly-made moss baskets retain their fresh green colour for some time, but eventually fade to a pleasing beige.

CHOOSING THE SETTING

This arrangement is best appreciated from above, so a coffee table or small occasional table would be ideal. Because the arrangement is so low, it would also be perfect for a dining table centre-piece, in the middle of a round or oval table. The criteria for a successful dinner-party flower arrangement is that it compliments the tablesetting and the decor of the room, without being too flamboyant or intrusive. An arrangement which is too tall, will inhibit the guests conversation. Another important factor for any dinner table arrangement is to make sure that the flowers' scent does not clash with the food.

If you have a conservatory, it would give a tropical, summery touch to a party held there, whatever the time of year. If displaying the basket on a sideboard that is set right up against a wall, turn the basket round the other way occasionally so that the wall-facing side can be admired too. Hippeastrums are the predominant flowers on one side while on the other, nerines steal the show.

DISPLAYING FRESH FLOWERS IN A MOSSY BASKET

YOU WILL NEED

1 *3 sprays chrysanthemum stems*
2 *6-7 nerine stems*
3 *hippeastrum flowerheads*
4 *2 bunches peach-coloured statice*
5 *5 stems alstroemeria*
6 *3 fatsia leaves*
7 *3 pittosporum stems*
8 *floristry scissors*
9 *florist's foam block*
10 *lined moss-covered basket*

1

2

3

4

5

6

1 Line the basket if necessary, then soak a florist's foam block and trim it to fit inside the basket. Wipe three fatsia leaves with a damp cloth, to clean them, then cut the leaf stalks back to 7.5cm (3in). Insert the leaves into the foam around the basket rim.

2 Cut three hippeastrum flowers under the flowerhead, leaving a little of the thick stem attached. Position the flowers in a tight clump, where one end of the handle meets the basket. Face the flowers outwards and upwards, for all-round interest. Hippeastrums bruise easily, so handle them with care.

3 Cut three stems of spray chrysanthemums back to about 7.5cm (3in), cutting at an angle, for ease of insertion. Insert the stems in a roughly circular area next to the hippeastrums, so that the chrysanthemums form a dense mass.

4 Shorten the statice stems, then bunch the flowers tightly in your hand. Insert into the foam block, from the chrysanthemums round to the handle. Use the statice to form a roughly rounded wedge. Cut the alstroemeria flowers into individual stalks, and make a dense clump next to the statice.

5 Cut the pittosporum stems into small sprigs, 10-15cm (4-6in) long. Build up a tight clump of pittosporum between the alstroemeria and statice, following the rounded contours of the display. The foliage adds contrast and texture.

6 Finally, cut off the nerine flowers just below where the individual flower stalks meet the main stem. Remove the sepals. Tuck the flowers into the foam to form a dense clump just behind the pittosporum foliage and the alstroemeria.

STEP *by* STEP

Glass Containers

The unusual aspect of this informal arrangement of lilies, gerbera, lady's mantle and trachelium is the clever stem-holding device which uses bundles of cinnamon sticks to fill a clear glass vase. The spice bundles, interwoven with orange peel, surround the flower stems, holding them upright and firmly in the centre of the vase.

A TOUCH OF SPICE

Fruits and spices are used in cooking for their flavours and aromas. The featured display exploits the colour, texture and form of bunches of cinnamon in combination with fresh flowers and fruit. Oranges, here used for their peel, are available reasonably priced all year round. Old-fashioned cinnamon sticks, less popular than ground cinnamon, are also widely and cheaply available.

CHOOSING THE FLOWERS

All the flowers shown are available from florists, but some are easily-grown garden flowers, and there are many possible substitutes. Whatever the combination of flowers you choose, try to include some that are daisy-shaped, others that are trumpet-shaped and delicate flowers and flat-headed blooms for good contrast of form and outline.

Gerbera, or the Transvaal daisy, is a South-African member of the daisy family, named after the German botanist, Dr Gerber. A pale apricot variety is shown, but gerberas come in almost every shade and tint of yellow, orange and red, as well as lilac and pure white. There are single and double forms, too, and many flower-heads have contrasting central zones or discs.

Few florists stock more than two or three gerbera varieties at any one time, so order in advance to be sure of obtaining your chosen colour. If gerberas are not available, use shasta daisies, pyrethrums, annual sunflowers, cosmos, coreopsis or single florist's chrysanthemums. They are all just as suitable because they have a similar shape.

SEASONAL LILIES

Lilies are available from florists all year round but in late summer, garden lilies are at their most prolific. Choose from tiger lilies, golden-ray lilies, Japanese lilies and Turk's cap lilies. Most florist's and garden lilies are suitable for this display, although Easter-type lilies are too large for an arrangement on this scale. In addition some people find the scent of certain lilies unpleasant; for example, Turk's cap lily has a strong, musky scent.

The creamy-white lilies used in the featured display are chosen to complement the apricot-coloured gerberas. Instead of using large lilies, for a more delicate effect, use multi-flowered pink Guernsey nerine or Peruvian lilies (alstroemeria), or the beautiful blue umbels of agapanthus.

COOL-LOOK FLOWERS

Lady's mantle is an easy-to-grow, herbaceous perennial plant. Its clear, lime-green flowers last well in arrangements. Fortunately, lady's mantle is now being grown and sold commercially for the cut-flower trade. As an alternative to lady's mantle, use massed bunches of gypsophila, astilbe, meadowsweet or meadow rue. If necessary, take the large flowerheads apart and display in smaller, shorter sections.

Mauve trachelium, or throatwort, adds contrasting form and cool colour, but probably will have to be ordered in advance from the florist. If your colour scheme allows, substitute the flat, golden-yellow flowerheads of achillea or rich, russet sedum or valerian.

Ivy leaves provide the filler foliage. Ivy grows plentifully in the garden and is sold as foliage material at most florists. Choose mature leaves and condition them by submerging in water for a few hours before arranging.

CHOOSING THE FRUIT AND SPICES

An orange peel is shown but lemon, lime, satsuma, clementine, tangerine or grapefruit peel could be substituted. For greater colour interest, use the peels of two different citrus fruit, interweaving them in the bundles of cinnamon: lemon and orange, grapefruit and lime, or orange and lime all make attractive combinations.

Cinnamon sticks are made from the bark of the tropical cinnamon tree. Often, cinnamon peel is used whole, in drinks, such as mulled wine, or cooked with stewed, dried fruits, such as apricots and prunes. For details on how to make the cinnamon bundles see the tinted box. The cinnamon bundles are very light so may float in the vase water. Anchor them with reel wire to a small stone or insert them into a layer of florist's adhesive clay in the bottom of the vase; make sure the vase is totally dry before attempting this, or the clay will not adhere to the base.

CHOOSING THE CONTAINER

A clear glass container is essential to see the attractive stem-holding devices. The fluted vase has special character and charm, but a short, straight-sided glass vase can be used instead. Make sure the vase is perfectly clean before you start; scouring with lemon juice or vinegar and salt is an old-fashioned, but effective, way of removing stains from glass. To make a miniature version of the same display, place a few cinnamon stick bundles in an ordinary glass drinking tumbler, and proceed as for the larger arrangement. You could make several arrangements in glass vases of different dimensions and shapes to be displayed together. Use clear rather than coloured glass containers to maximize the impact of the fruit, perhaps placing different fruits in each.

CHOOSING THE SETTING

You could expand on the culinary theme and display the arrangement in the kitchen or dining room, though it would make

CINNAMON BUNDLES

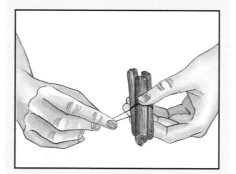

Group together three perfect cinnamon sticks, staggering them slightly. Wrap a short length of reel wire around each bundle. Twist the wire ends together securely, but not too tightly as this may cause the cinnamon sticks to crack and shatter. Make about ten bundles in all or enough to fill your vase.

This distinctly different flower display is set in clear glass vase and distinguished further by the unusual holding mechanics. (ABOVE)

just as good a focal point in a living room or conservatory. For a profusion of colour in a hallway or other spacious setting, you might group two or three such arrangements together. Always position any such displays where they cannot be accidentally knocked over and will not cause an obstruction.

LOOKING AFTER THE DISPLAY

Spray-mist the flowers daily, especially in hot, dry weather and change the vase water regularly. The simplest way of achieving this without disturbing your design is to spread out the fingers of both your hands round the stems and over the

rim, then tilt the vase gently over the sink, allowing the water to spill out but keeping the stems in position. Return it to an upright position, fill with fresh water and readjust the flowers as necessary. Remove the lower lilies as they fade. You will also find that the display is likely to last for longer if you place it well away from any draughts and also keep it out of direct sunlight.

When it comes to taking apart the display, cut off the lower stems of lady's mantle, loosely bunch the flowers, and hang them upside-down to air dry.

Don't throw away any flowers that still have life in them; cut them off carefully and use them in a miniature display.

DISPLAYING FRUIT AND FLOWERS IN A VASE

YOU WILL NEED

 1 *3 stems of trachelium*
 2 *8-10 stems of lady's mantle*
 3 *2 lily stems*
 4 *4 stems of gerbera*
 5 *10 ivy leaves*
 6 *30 cinnamon sticks*
 7 *1 orange*
 8 *reel wire*
 9 *floristry scissors*
 10 *clear glass vase*

1

2

3

4

5

6

1 Make up ten cinnamon bundles (see page 65). Fill the centre of the vase with the spice bundles. They may float, so anchor them with reel wire wrapped round a small stone. Half-fill the vase with water, do not dislodge the bundles.

2 Cut a length of rind from one orange, about 1.5cm (½in) wide. Remove any pith. Divide the peel into three or four sections. Interweave the end of each section between the cinnamon bundles. Allow some of the peel to hang over the rim of the vase.

3 Cut three stems of trachelium so that the flowerheads stand at least 6cm (2½in) above the rim of the vase. Group the trachelium stems so that the flowerheads are bunched together. Position them slightly to one side of the vase.

4 Trim two lily stems, so that the uppermost bud is about twice the height of the vase. Strip away the lower leaves from each stem. Position the two lily stems in the centre of the vase so that the flowers appear to emerge from the grouped mass of trachelium flowerheads.

5 Cut four gerbera stems to the same height as the trachelium. Group them together on the opposite side of the vase to the trachelium. Wire together the short stems of two ivy leaves so they overlap slightly; make five wired pairs. Place around the edge of the vase to form a collar of foliage.

6 Remove between eight to ten sprays from three stems of lady's mantle. Strip the lower leaves from the stems. Intersperse throughout the other flowers to add a light and frothy touch to the display. Follow the dome shape created by the other plant material.

Exploring the Spectrum

BE CREATIVE WITH SHADES, HUES, TINTS AND TONES TO MAKE
THE MOST OF YOUR FLOWER ARRANGEMENTS.

A profusion of bright flowers blend together to give a harmonious and pleasing arrangement. (FAR RIGHT)

In perfect harmony is a term that is often applied to flower arrangements. Different people may find completely different colour blends pleasing. One person may enjoy a melody of green and yellow foliage with a trio of golden gerberas as the focal point. Another's favourite colour combination might be rich warm hues, interpreted perhaps in spicy red carnations, coral freesias and bright orange lilies.

In colour terms, both of these mixtures would be considered harmonious – and both would be pleasing to the eye. The colour wheel, which is used by flower arrangers, artists, designers – in fact everyone who uses colour for decorative effect – is the key to creating colour harmony.

A LOOK AT THE SPECTRUM

The colour wheel, in its simplest form, is divided into six segments. The three alternate sections are the primary colours: red, yellow and blue. Between them are the secondary colours which are made by mixing the two primaries on either side. Therefore, orange is between the primary colours red and yellow, green between yellow and blue, and mauve between blue and red. It is easy to remember which colours harmonize together: any three colours adjacent on the colour wheel constitute harmonizing colours; those which are directly opposite each other are termed 'contrasting'.

For example, it is because yellow and green are next to each other on the colour wheel that green and yellow foliage,

sharpened with bright yellow flowers, would look so harmonious. Another example is red and orange which also are adjacent colours, creating harmony in a hot and spicy arrangement of summer flowers.

Blend any three colours next to each other on the wheel and reveal the variety of shades that can be achieved. There are not only six colours, or hues as they are called. Every colour has a pale tint, which is the basic hue mixed with white; a tone, which is the basic colour blended with grey; and a shade, when it is mixed with black.

For a 'red' harmony, use the palest, softest sugar pink tints of paeonies or roses; the middle tones of, for example, phlox and astilbes, and the deep shades of dark red gladioli and sweet williams. Combine these lovely garden flowers together in a large red china jug, and still only one colour has been used.

IN TUNE WITH CONTAINERS

When aiming to reproduce the special effects of harmonious flower colour in displays, the container holding the arrangement also must be taken into account. The result could be altered totally – although not necessarily spoiled – by your choice of container colour. For example, a display could still look impressive if blue, mauve and red flowers were arranged in an enamel bowl of a fourth colour, yellow. With all the flowers in complete harmony – all blending into

𝒫ink, red and orange combine perfectly in this arrangement of gerberas, carnations and alstroemeria. The bright fruit emphasizes the effect of the flower composition. (BELOW)

each other — the first thing to be seen would be the striking yellow container. Like eyes adjusting to brilliant sunshine, it would take some time before it is noticed that the mound of flowers consisted of, for example, blue and purple pansies, mauve scabious and red pyrethrums. In contrast, a container in any one of the colours of the featured flowers, whether it is a pale tint, a medium tone or a deep shade, would

blend perfectly and serve to unify the arrangement.

Another illustration of colours fighting for attention would be a selection of flowers in the golden hues of autumn, such as yellow, orange and red zinnias or godetias, which are arranged in a blue vase. Blue is opposite orange on the colour wheel and has no other colour in common visually with the flowers. Once again, the container would dominate the arrangement, whereas a copper jug, varnished willow basket or wooden container would not draw attention away from the flowers themselves.

BALANCING HUES

The depth of colour and the way it is used has a significant effect on the appearance of an arrangement. Strong, dark, rich shades can have a heavy appearance. A pale pastel pink container used to display dark red flowers might look as if it is being squashed under the visual weight of the colours. A blend of perfectly harmonious flowers, such as lime-green tobacco plant flowers, pale green zinnias, light blue scabious and deep mauve irises, with all the darkest purple flowers at the top of the design may appear top heavy. Placing some of the darkest flowers at the base, close to the centre of the arrangement, will add visual stability — or what some arrangers refer to as 'colour ballast'.

In any mixture of flower colours, however well matched and harmonious, some of them will predominate. The way to judge is to hold up the bunch, half-close your eyes, and see which flowers seem to prevail over the others. In any group, these flowers are likely to be white, bright, sharp yellow, deep red, blue, purple, or brown. Which ones play this leading role will depend on the colour balance of the rest of the group.

These predominant flowers are the ones that need watching. If they are positioned at random throughout, the result is unlikely to be graceful and harmonious. This is because, at first, the eye will be drawn to these flowers. If the predominant flowers are placed with no apparent thought, the design may look awkward and discordant.

The solution is to place these powerful colours so they make an easy, rhythmic shape; for example, a gently curving 'S' shape ranging from the top to the bottom

of the arrangement, with a group of the eye-catching flowers close to the centre base. The dominant flowers could follow two or three curves which would give an interesting, structured striped effect instead of a random, dotted look.

HARMONIOUS SURROUNDINGS

When creating a flower arrangement, unless it is designed to be taken on to the terrace or out into the garden, it will be appreciated more if it blends in with the furnishings and is in complete harmony with the surrounding room decor. A design with flowers and container in complete harmony can still look out of place if not in keeping with the room setting.

Patterns and colours of a room often instigate exciting ideas for flower designs. It is not only the principal furnishings and the main colour schemes that can inspire special arrangements. It is possible to give quite different impressions by emphasising a colour combination or pattern from an accessory or a small piece of furniture.

Another way to use furnishings for motivation is to pick up just one colour in the curtains, carpet or wallpaper, make that a focal point of the flower arrangement and then expand into another colour direction. For example, bright orange gerberas, and paler orange carnations could echo the colour of broad bands in a fabric or rug. Instead of picking up the browns and blues which might make up the rest of the material – and which could look dull in further repetition – the flowers should be much brighter. By introducing vibrant red and pink, colours which are in harmony with the orange, the flower design is lifted. In addition, the use of white flowers would help to separate each of these vivid colours. The resultant display would still harmonize with its surroundings.

But do remember that it is not just the flower colouring that you should consider. The style of display is just as important as the individual flowers and your general colour scheme. Think carefully about whether you want to go for a traditional, formal style or whether another approach would be more appropriate.

The two ginger jars, one in a traditional Chinese pattern and the other a blend of blue, green and mauve, provide the tonal key for these informal flower arrangements. (ABOVE)

CREATING A MOOD

Clever blending with your floral palette creates many moods from cool and distant to fiery and forceful.

This orange, textured pottery vase with a loose bouquet of late summer flowers in hot hues makes a bold feature for a living room. (RIGHT)

Dip into your floral paintbox to create dazzling displays in bold mixes of contrasting shades. (FAR RIGHT)

Flower compositions in contrasting hues are eye-catching and dynamic. Bright red pyrethrums and sweet peas nestling among glossy green leaves and pale green nicotiana flowers; purple and yellow pansies floating in a bowl; gentian-blue alkanet and sky-blue borage paired with a handful of sunny marigolds – all these colourful partnerships will attract attention from family and friends.

Combinations of contrasting coloured flowers can be used when you want to give a room a new flash of design inspiration; when you want to create a different effect for a party or special occasion, perhaps, or simply boost your spirits. A stunning basket of purple and golden flowers displayed on a table in front of a window, for instance, will evoke warmth and sunshine and really brighten up a miserable day.

INSPIRED COMBINATIONS

Discover new, bold combinations by drawing inspiration from items around you. You may have an accessory in the home that is full of the colours that would look arresting together in a flower arrangement; it may never have occurred to you to combine them in the same vase.

It doesn't have to be the brightest towel on the beach that inspires you to combine

CREATING IMPACT

The special impact that you make with arrangements in deliberately contrasting colours works only if you use those colours in profusion. A miniature design packed with midnight-blue lobelia and burnt-orange tagetes will have style because, in such close proximity, each flower type will complement the colour in the other. Don't make the mistake of scattering small flowers in clashing colours randomly through a large design as it will only result in a distracting effect not a bold statement.

A design composed of orange dahlias and blue irises would look casual and stylish, especially if the large blooms were arranged in colour clusters, lines or curves. A design made up of many small or medium-sized flowers, however, would make an impact only if the flowers were arranged in groups. Some flowers, of course, are so big, bold and beautiful that they don't need this kind of treatment to catch the eye and hold the attention. Anthuriums, for example, with their bold red colour and eye-catching shape always make a major impact. Golden yellow sunflowers also merit their own display.

DIFFERENT MOODS

Colour schemes in a floral display can greatly influence the ambience of a room. Certain colours can create a soothing atmosphere, whilst others are more likely to tire the eyes if they are looked at for long periods of time. Consider the effects of different colours when you are planning a display, so that you can create an arrangement appropriate to its setting.

The range of blue colours tends to be regarded as the cool hues. In a room which faces south and is flooded with sunlight, blue flowers can have a cooling effect. During the winter months, an abundance of blue in the decor of a north-facing room can create a chilly atmosphere. The featured blue floral display suggests the gentle sadness of 'feeling blue'. The shades of blue blend together with the basket, towels, shells and other accessories, setting a gentle, yet melancholy mood.

Red, on the other hand, is a bold and commanding colour which is hard to ignore. Red engenders warmth; it can be a welcoming colour as well as a warning of danger. However, if red is over-used, it

A cool look is created with a vase lined with frosty-looking fragmented glass and refreshing blue and white flowers. (ABOVE)

bold colours. An everyday item, such as a random patchwork cushion, may have an unusual juxtaposition of colour – perhaps a particular shade of blue that you usually would not consider combining with a particular tone of orange. If the colours work well in the fabric, they probably will suit a flower arrangement.

An observant flower arranger will be inspired by all manner of things. You may be in an art gallery, looking at a poster, choosing a greetings card or admiring a child's painting. Make the most of such experiences to give you ideas for your own compositions. Once you start looking around you and discovering new and dramatic mixes of colour, you will feel free to ignore restrictive adages such as 'blue and green should ne'er be seen' – whoever made this remark originally had probably never seen a field of vibrant, beautiful bluebells!

Not all arrangements need to be bold to create a mood. The soft pinks and greens in this arrangement combine to give a softer, more tranquil effect. (LEFT)

The bright red ceramic container and the china bull enhance the vivid red flowers, creating a vibrant, bold mood. (LEFT)

Blue hydrangeas, larkspur, statice and eryngium are used to create an air of melancholy and nostalgia. (FAR LEFT)

can create a restless and disturbing atmosphere. In the featured arrangement, red roses, gladioli and *Berberis thunbergii* 'Atropurpurea' are displayed together, creating a vibrant, daring effect which works extremely well.

Yellow is always associated with warmth. A few yellow flowers in a small bunch make a suitable gift for a hospital patient. A pale yellow decor gives a room a constant warmth which can be enhanced by an arrangement of rich golden blooms and foliage.

Purple can create very different moods, depending on the colours with which it is arranged. For example, if purple flowers are arranged with flamboyant red ones, they take on a warm look, but in juxtaposition with blue flowers, the purple becomes a cool and rich colour.

STEP *by* STEP

Creating a Mood

Be adventurous with your flower arrangements and see how bold splashes of vibrant colour can create a vibrant, exciting effect. This arrangement of bright summer flowers will give a lift to any room in your home, and it's eye-catching enough to feature at a special occasion.

CHOOSING THE FLOWERS
The colours of the selected flowers are intense – bright pink gerberas and deep-yellow ranunculus – for a jazzy modern look. However, if your heart is set on softer colours, you can tone down the shades and achieve equally beautiful results in a different mood. White hydrangeas, white gerberas and creamy-white ranunculus, for example, would give a cool, sophisticated display; or, if you prefer, try putting pink hydrangeas, pink gerberas and pink ranunculus together for a softly feminine scheme.

The colours you eventually choose will, of course, be somewhat affected by what is available at the florist or in your garden. Even though it's a good idea to have in mind the colour scheme you particularly want, try to be flexible if your find that flowers are not available in the shades that you had set your heart on. In other words, always be ready to adapt and change the colours, if necessary.

A MODERN VASE
We have used a modern, white glazed china vase, roughly triangular in plan and about 20cm (8 in) across. The sides are angled outwards slightly, and the free-form, curving base creates an attractive, undulating effect. You may not be able to find an exact replica, but any tall, straight-sided or outward-angled container can be used instead, provided it has a reasonably wide neck. As well as white, you could use china glazed in a single bright colour, perhaps repeating

CONDITIONING HYDRANGEAS

Hydrangea flowers will last longer in the vase if water can be drawn up the stems easily. This won't hapen if they are exposed to the air for any length of time, the stem end begins to heal over and is sealed gradually by a protective callus. This prevents water from entering the stem, thus causing the flower to wilt prematurely.

Remove the seal by plunging the stem end in a few inches of boiling water. This kills those cells immersed in the water and prevents them from becoming a callus. Protect the flowerhead from the heat of the steam by covering it with a cloth or bag. Leave the stems to cool in a deep container of water before arranging. Keep cut hydrangeas fresh with regular spray-misting.

Big blooms in bright tints make a bold and beautiful display. (FAR RIGHT)

one of the flower colours, or a modern glass cube or cylinder vase. If you use a glass container, pay special attention to the appearance of the stems and remove all of the leaves that will fall below the water-line.

The main challenge of a wide-necked container, such as the one shown, is to keep stems upright. Florist's foam and crumpled chickenwire are traditional supports, but here, clear sticky tape is criss-crossed over the rim, forming an almost invisible webbing to hold the stems in place. It's perfect for a glass container as nothing shows, or for a delicate or valuable container which would be damaged by chickenwire.

For a modern container that suits most contemporary settings, a reliable standby is a plain black or white cylindrical vase. This will complement and suit even the boldest of flowers.

CHOOSING THE SETTING

A bright splash of flower colur will bring any indoor setting to life. The display is featured here in a modern living room against a neutral background which makes a perfect foil for the richly coloured blooms. If your home is furnished in a more traditional style, there is still a place for this type of flower design. Even the most delicate interior colour scheme often has tiny sparks of bright colour, such as the centre of flowers on a miniature-print wallpaper or fabric.

BRIGHT MODERN DISPLAY

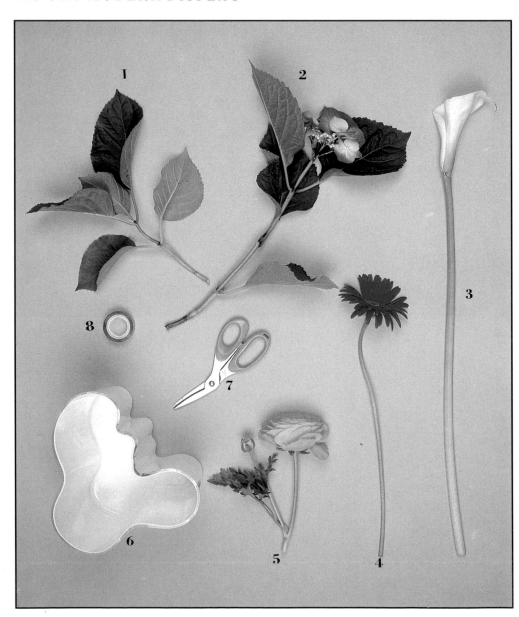

YOU WILL NEED

1 *3 stems of hydrangea foliage*
2 *3 blue hydrangea flowers*
3 *3 stems of arum lily*
4 *4 stems of pink gerbera*
5 *3 stems of yellow ranunculus*
6 *vase*
7 *floristry scissors*
8 *sticky tape*

1

2

3

4

5

6

1 Fill the vase two-thirds full with water. Following the curves of the vase across the top, divide it into four sections with criss-cross strips of clear sticky tape. Cut the tape to length so that the ends are not visible over the edge of the vase.

2 Cut the ends of three stems of hydrangea leaves that have no flowers. Cut the stems to one and half times the height of the vase. The hydrangea foliage provides the basic framework and gives support. Place the stems in the two middle sections so they lean on the sticky tape.

3 Cut the stems of three arum lilies at a slant in graduated lengths, the tallest one at least one flowerhead higher than the other two blooms. Place them against the back edge of the vase in a trio, with their stems standing completely straight.

4 Snip the ends of four bright-pink gerbera stems, keeping as much as possible of their length. Place all four flowers in one section at the side of the vase. Rest the flowers against each other and on to the strips of sticky tape, facing forwards.

5 Cut three leafy hydrangea stems to the same height as the other flowers. Group them in a taped-off section on the opposite side of the vase to the pink gerberas. Place two flowerheads leaning out sideways from the display and one flower more centrally, facing forwards.

6 Finish off with bright yellow ranunculus. Leave the stems at their full length. Place three flowers in a taped section in the central focal point to make a yellow group at the front of the display. Support the flowers with more hydrangea foliage if necessary.

Advanced Ideas with Flowers

EXPERIMENT WITH DIFFERENT APPROACHES AND BE BOLD WITH
MORE ELABORATE ACCESSORIES FOR YOUR ARRANGEMENTS.

*A family of natural
maize figures inspires a
still-life group with a country
air. The ears of corn scattered
around, throwing the tonal
spotlight on to the art
nouveau vase of brilliant red,
coral and pink nasturtiums.*
(ABOVE)

Accessory is a recognised term of reference in competitive flower arranging, and applies to any item not made of plant material which may be incorporated in, or grouped with, a flower arrangement exhibit. Items based on natural material, such as a carved figure or even a bird's nest, also count as accessories.

The most popular accessories used in flower arranging competitions are candles, feathers, figurines, stones and shells, but there are endless other possibilities. Containers, mechanics and background drapes are all seen as essentials, and therefore are allowed in competitive work which excludes accessories. When arranging for pleasure at home, however, there is no reason why you should not use drapes and create some stylish and attractive displays using fabric for both its texture and pattern.

CONVEYING A MESSAGE

Accessories can contribute greatly to flower arrangements. They can carry a symbolic message to convey the theme of an interpretative arrangement. This could be most appropriate at a gathering to mark a special occasion, such as a wedding, christening, Christmas or birthday party, or for festivals, such as harvest or Easter.

You can use accessories to provide interest when flowers are scarce or too expensive to buy in large numbers. You can also let them reinforce the line and colour of the arrangement in which they are to feature.

INCORPORATING ACCESSORIES

Candles, feathers, stones and shells may be put to good use within the arrangement itself. Figures and models are usually positioned next to the flowers, with a single base holding both in place and bringing unity to the display. There should be some obvious connection in line, colour or significance between the flowers and the accessory. Just placing a statue next to a bunch of flowers won't make an interpreted display unless there is a reason for the statue to be there.

Pay particular attention to scale, both in show work and when arranging for your own pleasure at home. Don't use accessories so small that they make no impact, or so large that the flowers pale into insignificance beside them. If you are considering using several accessories together, they must be in scale with each other – a huge butterfly and a small horse side by side would look incongruous.

You can be creative with perspective and bring smaller objects closer to the eye to make them appear larger, and vice versa. A useful point to bear in mind is that if you position the accessory before you start arranging, its inclusion is more likely to look deliberate rather than an afterthought.

CANDLES FOR ALL OCCASIONS

One of the most popular accessories is the Christmas or party candle. Candles and

An old copper corn and bean scoop, almost a cornucopia in shape, with a fanfare-type display of bronze and coral dahlias and blue water irises, highlights a collection of copper moulds and kitchen utensils. (LEFT)

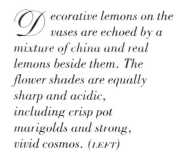

Decorative lemons on the vases are echoed by a mixture of china and real lemons beside them. The flower shades are equally sharp and acidic, including crisp pot marigolds and strong, vivid cosmos. (LEFT)

The simple apricot pattern of the bowl is echoed in the spray carnations, alternating in rings with spray chrysanthemum flowers. The matching duck provides an extra appeal to the display. (RIGHT)

flowers look good together at any special occasion. Although sometimes candles in flower designs are not intended to be lit, the transitory nature of both the blooms and the flame adds to the festive atmosphere of a celebration and also adds romance to an intimate dinner.

PARTY PIECES

Accessories can be significant, useful, beautiful or just good fun. At a children's party, colourful novelties and gifts for the young visitors can be incorporated amusingly into bunches of flowers to make the party table look bright and festive. Use the accessories as prizes for party games, to be admired during the birthday tea, and get the winner to pick his or her choice out of the arrangement without spoiling it.

Ideal presents that can be incorporated in simple flower displays held in chicken wire are party whistles, children's make-up sticks, coloured lollies and candy sticks of all kinds. Group them with bright, coloured flowers, such as nasturtiums, marigolds or any member of the daisy family. Choose something cheerful.

COFFEE TABLE DECORATIONS

Accessories displayed near flowers on low tables are in a good position to catch attention. This is just the place to put a little bowl of red roses in the middle of a large dish of red billiard balls for an amusing visual contrast, or to arrange sprays of sea holly and thrift in a sea shell.

NOSTALGIC ACCESSORIES

You can revive an old custom and create an arrangement in a flower bowl. These were particularly popular in the 1930s and the originals still can be found in junk shops and antique shops. The flower bowls themselves were wide and shallow, having a turned-in rim decorated perhaps with water-lilies or dragonflies. The idea was to float flowerheads in the bowl and

A glazed chintz, patterned with large pink flower trusses, complements a generous swathe of flowers in a single shade which is further embellished by the richly floral china. (LEFT)

stand a china model of an Oriental waterfowl or a woodpecker in the middle of it. The model itself would be pierced with holes and hollow inside, so that you could insert more flower stems down through the holes and into the water.

If you can't find the original ceramics, improvise with a shallow bowl and one or two china birds and animals. Alternatively, look out for an attractive hat-pin holder, which would serve equally well for holding flowers. Sweet peas look delightful in this kind of setting, and rose-buds floating on the water resemble miniature water-lilies. The use of twigs with a few green leaves completes the scene.

ENHANCING COLLECTIONS

Another way of using flowers with accessories is to look around your home and see whether an arrangement of fresh flowers could enhance a favourite collection.

A dressing table often holds private things, such as treasured photos in silver

The rich tapestry fabric combines with the pewter-type container to enrich the tones of the gerberas. (LEFT)

frames, and a group of old scent bottles in coloured glass. Place a vase at the back, in front of the mirror and fill it with delicate flowers – pink and white hydrangeas, love-in-a-mist and bridewort. Take a few individual stems and one or two leaves, and put them in your scent bottles.

ART AS INSPIRATION

*Take a cue from floral representations in your home
to compose elegant and stylish displays.*

*F̶estone di fiori e frutta
by J Davidsz van Heem
is a perfect example of a Dutch
old master that can be followed
to create a sumptuous
arrangement. (ABOVE)*

If you are short of arranging ideas and want to create a stunning display, try turning to art for inspiration and make your own fresh-flower 'masterpiece'.

Find new and interesting ways of combining flowers and foliage in arrangements by looking around you at fabrics, china, prints and paintings. Flowers are a very popular subject with artists and craftsmen of both the past and present, so there is a whole range of traditional and modern ideas for you to try.

An inspirational source of stunning flower displays are 17th-century Dutch still-life paintings. Visit any gallery or pick up an art book or catalogue and you will see many of these exquisitely-painted flower arrangements with fabulous combinations of large, exotic and garden blooms in beautiful urns and vases.

The Dutch artists had a free hand in the

flowers they chose to represent, regardless of their seasonal availability. They probably would not have seen them in life but drew them from model books. When adapting one of these paintings for a fresh-flower display you will therefore have to be fairly flexible in the flowers you use, and in some cases, find real-life alternatives to luxury or fantasy flowers. Today, many of the flowers the Dutch regarded as exotic blooms are available at the florist and we can create these glorious displays relatively inexpensively.

DUPLICATING ART

We have taken as our inspiration a painting by Ambrosins Bosschaert, the Younger and used his colourful spring combination of paeonies, tulips, irises, lilies and narcissi.

As the basis for our design, we have chosen a similar round glass bowl, interesting to the artist and arranger for its potential to reflect light. We have also taken the simple triangular shape of the display and placed the long-stemmed flowers at the top and fuller, more open flowers towards the rim of the vase. The painter has used a great deal of artistic licence in creating his arrangement, where tulips stand upright without any holding props at all! In a real display you will have to use florist's tape, laid in a criss-cross network of strips across the rim to support the flower stems. As far as possible we have attempted to capture the spirit of the painting by placing similar flowers in the same positions.

If you want to create more modern, expressionistic displays, turn to the flower paintings of the Post-Impressionists and the Symbolists. Identifying specific flowers is often difficult — try instead to recapture a similar mood or feeling in your arrangement through the intense colours of the flowers and mixed textures.

Flowers have inspired many great

artists over the years. As you have seen, the wonderful still life groupings by 17th-century Dutch masters, such as van Huysum and Kessel, display profusions of summer flowers with the detailed texture of each petal so life-like that they give the impression of being in the room with you. The soft, pastel coloured paintings of the French Impressionists, such as Monet's visionary water lilies floating in a lake of sparkling blue, or his yellow irises, vibrant against pink clouds, can also inspire you to create delicate new arrangements.

If you are a flower enthusiast, it is more than likely that you have framed prints of flowers hanging on your wall, or perhaps you are lucky enough to own some flower paintings, or even talented enough to paint them yourself. But even if you are not artistically inclined, you can pay tribute to the artist by making a flower arrangement to complement the picture by putting them side by side. You will find the effect very eye-catching and it gives the picture a three dimensional feel as your room becomes part of the picture.

ROOM REPRODUCTIONS

If you enjoy this effect, it might be something that you bear in mind next time you decorate your room. You could create a Van Gogh bedroom, with twin beds of yellow wood, blue bedclothes and a scrubbed board floor, a rush seated chair

and, of course, a pot of giant yellow sunflowers. Or a sitting room depicted by the Expressionist painter Matisse, with yellow and grey striped walls, a pink velvet armchair, and a blue and white Chinese pot of brilliant anemones on a small marble-topped table. Arrange the flowers loosely and scatter a handful of golden kumquats next to them on a table. Then delight in the surprise of visitors as they look around the room, then at the picture on the wall, then back again in amazement.

If you have a flower picture, the best idea is to follow as closely as possible which flowers the picture illustrates. If this can't be managed, perhaps because the flowers are out of season, or you can't quite make out what type they are, simply pick out the dominant colour of the painted flower and copy the shape of the bunch.

A graphic example of how to achieve the look of a painting in a floral arrangement. (ABOVE)

SIMPLE STYLE

You can create a stunning tableau if you have a richly detailed still life painting hanging above a lovely old sideboard of glowing wood. Choose an urn of the right shape, whether it is delicately patterned or plain white. To get the required height, you might need to crumple chicken wire to the rim of the vase then place the florist's foam on top. Now build up a luxurious arrangement following the picture behind: it might contain pink lilies, montbretia, pink larkspur, Michaelmas daisies, berberis, fennel, pink roses and sweet chestnut leaves. Position the arrangement on the sideboard or a shelf near to its painted twin where it does not obscure it, and look to see what else you can incorporate from the picture into the still life. Perhaps a shallow crystal dish laden with mauve grapes, pomegranates and peaches would complement it. Many pictures feature fallen petals or fruits that have spilled over from the dish, and you could incorporate these touches.

MODERN INTERPRETATIONS

Any picture can provide inspiration for arranging flowers even if it does not depict them. Moving from the extravagant to the simple, take a stark, modern interior that is mainly black and white. You are more likely to have a geometric pattern in a frame than a bunch of flowers, but you can still echo the spirit of the painting. If the artist has created unusual shapes and spaces without the use of colour, then you

*I*n this modern room, the airiness depicted in the large print is echoed in two simple and delicate arrangements, as well as by the houseplants and the ivy outside. (*RIGHT*)

Flower arrangements that are inspired by paintings do not have to be traditional to be strikingly effective – as this modern interpretation shows. (LEFT)

can follow his lead. Look for a very simple vase – a cylindrical or rectangular shape in chrome, black or white ceramic or glass, and choose flowers that make a bold statement, such as white lilies.

Other flowers that look good in modern settings include anthuriums and bird of paradise flowers (strelitzia), both chosen for their exotic colours and dramatic shapes, or simply select large white daisies, especially gerberas. The classic shape of the daisy is often the first flower children ever draw.

DOUBLE TAKES

You can have great fun with flowers and trompe l'œil (artistic illusion). If you are thinking of decorating a wall with a mural painting or embellishing your furniture with flowers, look in your garden if your have one, for flowers to copy in paint or fabric. Choose flowers that grow in profusion and which have a long flowering season, alternatively if you have not got a garden, choose your favourite florist's flower. It must be something you particularly enjoy having in the house or which is easily available to use as a permanent feature as once you have gone to the effort of painting it you want to be certain you won't tire of it quickly! When you have painted your wall or piece of furniture,

This arrangement shows a stunning combination of golden rod, tansy, hypericum and chrysanthemums set against a work of art, in this instance a tapestry, depicting a similar mix of vivid hues. (RIGHT)

finish your room with strategically placed bunches of the real thing. No-one will be able to look at it without marvelling at the ingenious effect.

SMALLER EFFORTS

If you are not confident enough to paint a mural, you could begin with something smaller, such as a dining hatch. Select a vase that looks good on the shelf and fill it with flowers that fit comfortably into the recess, but leave some space to one side. Now paint on to the hatch a picture of your vase of flowers standing on a windowsill. Concentrate on the flowers – the background can be left as a wash of white emulsion paint. Prepare your surface so it is dirt-free and apply the white emulsion. When it is dry, outline the flowers in pencil. Fill them in with acrylic colours available from any art shop. It does not matter if you aren't a great artist; the point is that it is colourful, eye-catching and your own design. You will be delighted when you place the vase of flowers next to the painted one and admire the effect you have created. You could try this effect on any small wall panel or recess.

Alternatively, choose a piece of furniture with panels. Decorate a blanket trunk or an old upright piano. Paint your piano dark blue or green and place on the top a row of jugs filled with vividly coloured fresh flowers, such as nasturtiums, marigolds, roses or sweet peas, to create a massed effect. Now copy these bunches, in their jugs, by painting them on to the panels beneath.

TAPESTRY TEXTURE

If you are taking the inspiration for your flower arrangement from a tapestry or embroidery rather than a flat picture, then texture becomes important.

A suitable arrangement to complement an old tapestry would be a tray design depicting a hedgerow, set in a shallow terracotta dish. Build up the dish first with dry foam, and then cover it with silver lichen. Stud the foreground with ears of corn, wired then bent forward to represent the edge of a field, then make the 'hedgerow' with a combination of rich golden leaves on the turn, berries such as hawthorn, and billowy fronds of old man's beard. This will make a charming extension of the rustic scene woven into the tapestry.

A display of hawthorn berries with some leaves on the turn stands in a copper pot before a wall painting of equal richness. Intensity of tone and detail are the common links. (*LEFT*)

*R*oses and single daisy-flowered chrysanthemums copy the stylized daisies and poppies in the picture behind. The simple, cylindrical white pot complements the modern kitchen design. (*LEFT*)

A House
Full of Flowers

*N**o part of the kitchen need be dull – fresh flowers will transform even dark corners. (BELOW LEFT)*

*T**he dining end of a family kitchen looks more homely with flowers on the table. (BELOW RIGHT)*

Kitchens

A vase of fresh flowers displayed in the kitchen is both cheering and relaxing. Don't dismiss the idea of arranging flowers for the kitchen as being too time-consuming. The kitchen is not the place for complicated arrangements which look out of place in a busy environment.

Since part of the reason for having flowers in the kitchen is to bring a suggestion of sunshine indoors, choose blooms in light, bright, cheerful colours.

Unfussy containers are the best choice for kitchen displays. Pottery and glass jugs and mugs, teapots and coffee pots – any practical containers look at home in a busy working kitchen.

Living Rooms

When arranging flowers for your living room, decide what kind of impression you wish to create before you start. Whichever look you choose may depend as much on your mood as on the furnishings and decor of your room.

In a restful chintz room choose complementary colours of cream, pink, apricot and lavender with a touch of green to forge a link with the garden. The flowers should be soft; a combination of delicate, feathery and perfumed blooms that marry together perfectly – avoid anything spiky or garish that would strike a jarring note.

In a crowded family living room where no one colour dominates, you could make a colourful display of painted narrowboat jugs on the mantelpiece and fill them randomly with a selection of flowers.

A totally different look is called for in a modern living room. Here is your chance to be precise and sophisticated in your flower-arranging skills. Vases must be matching and streamlined. Two vases placed either end of the mantelpiece look good and balance each other.

Vases should be neutral in colour and

preferably plain. Use dramatic flowers like lilies or honesty, or use brightly coloured blooms, such as gerbera.

For a low table arrangement in a modern room, try a black bowl of bright gazania. Use grey-green foliage to emphasise the visual heat and intensity of the flowers and contrast with the bowl.

Flowers, flowers everywhere complement this elegant apricot and white sitting room. (LEFT)

Tea by a window overlooking the garden. The arrangement matches the occasion – a pottery basket of pinks, single chrysanthemums, and yellow heads of fennel flowers, with scented pelargonium leaves to add to the blend of aromas. (BELOW LEFT)

A handsome pair of terracotta vases holding gladioli look dramatic on a plain mantelpiece, while on the occasional table an informal display of dianthus and alstroemeria, secured in foam, brings vitality to this neutral room. (BELOW)

Room Corners

All too often, room corners can lack the visual impact of focal points such as tables, the fireplace and windows. Whether furniture is arranged around the walls or in the centre of the room, corners are often underlit, and visually uninspiring. Corners may also be the only areas of a room free from furniture or out of the reach of young children. As such, they are ideal for arrangements.

Enhance a sitting room corner by introducing a small pedestal table and use this to support a display of fresh flowers. Make sure the arrangement is placed above the level of chairs so that it is visible at all times.

If a room corner is slightly cheerless, try using pale-coloured flowers in your displays. The combination of pastel colours and glossy petals is especially effective and will lift a dull corner.

Another trick to brighten a dark area is to use white or very pale containers.

A collection of white crockery and a white fan-shaped container for the daffodil and iris arrangement dispels the shadows of a dark sitting room corner. (FAR RIGHT)

There is little natural light in this corner so light flowers are called for. White lilies in a painted container and cream spider chrysanthemums speckled with white gypsophila will attract attention. (RIGHT)

Stairways

Stairways, halls, passages and landings tend to be overlooked when it comes to planning flower arrangements. This is a pity, especially since flowers can enhance what may otherwise be a purely functional part of the house.

Staircases need large containers that will not look lost and that are sturdy if they get knocked. An appropriate choice would be an earthenware jug or pitcher or, for a really impressive result, an umbrella stand. If you use an umbrella stand, check that it is water-tight and, if necessary, stand a large pot or jar inside. Any container with a wide neck should be fitted just below the rim with crumpled wire netting to hold the stems.

If you have a small ledge on a passage wall, there may just be enough space for an arrangement in a narrow container. Also, remember that an arrangement placed close to a mirror will look twice as impressive when reflected in the glass.

A fragrant group of white lilies at the foot of the stairs tones with the neutral scheme of the sitting room. It provides a dramatic focal point in an area which is usually overlooked. (ABOVE)

This luscious arrangement of pink and red flowers graces any stairway, spiral or otherwise. (LEFT)

A basket of lush foliage brings the countryside indoors, while lace curtains filter harsh light. The vase of exuberant lilies decorates and enhances the whole room. (RIGHT)

Bedrooms

Formal and fussy flower arrangements seem out of place in a bedroom. Flowers here are prettiest when they are gathered together simply. Choose gentle salmon and peach tones rather than harsh pinks and smudge arrangements with feathery foliage. For a cool fresh look use violet, blue and green flowers.

Containers should reflect the mood of the room. Choose vases for their simplicity and unless you have a very large room, blend your arrangements with the colours and fabrics rather than contrasting patterns and tones.

Don't overlook the mood and shape of your furniture. A vase of lilies can look sensational reflected in a dressing table mirror, while a pitcher filled with blossom and tulips adds rustic charm.

When friends or relatives come to stay, the way in which a guest bedroom is decorated plays a significant part in creating a relaxed atmosphere. Place two or three subtle floral touches where visitors will appreciate them.

The morning sun lights up the blue and white pitcher filled with fruit blossom, doronicum and golden tulips, making the flowers shine in this pretty bedroom. (RIGHT)

Bathrooms

Some of the smartest and most luxurious bathrooms lack just one thing – a touch of warmth and colour. It is easy to get carried away, with buying co-ordinating tiles and fittings, towels and other furnishings and create a room in such perfect colour harmony that the result can lack interest and look almost dull.

Flowers are the easiest and prettiest way of adding a splash of colour to a bathroom. A tiled windowsill, like an alcove in an all-tiled wall, could be a natural frame for an exuberant burst of floral colour. In a grey and white room, it could be a large jug spilling over with yellow tulips with just a touch of gypsophila to link it with the room theme. The golden flowers would brighten up the room instantly, as if the sun had come out.

Blue is popular in bathrooms but it also can look uninvitingly cold. Yellow or green combined with blue makes both colours look unwelcoming and chilly. A vase of bright orange Chinese lanterns, a jug of marigolds beside the handbasin, a pot of marmalade-coloured zinnias or venidium, sometimes called Monarch of the Veldt, would all help to add warmth to such a bathroom. An important thing to remember when planning arrangements for the bathroom is that as they are subject to fluctuations in temperature and humidity, you will need to choose the hardiest of flowers to display in this situation. A suitable selection would include: chrysanthemums, carnations, and most bulbs.

A bathroom window shelf is an ideal place to display a tub of golden tulips. Even in the subdued lighting, the flowers are a vibrant addition to the bathroom. The tulip stems are cut to different lengths. (LEFT)

Dramatic cream gerberas set in a ring of glossy variegated ivy leaves make a stylish composition in a cream water jug. (BELOW LEFT)

A tall clear glass vase contains a casual arrangement of long-stemmed blooms which picks up the purple, green and white floral stencilling of the bathroom furnishings. (BELOW)

Index